Brazil Struggles for Development

A

Brazil Struggles for Development

GORDON CAMPBELL

Charles Knight & Co. Ltd.
London
1972

Charles Knight & Co. Ltd.
11-12 Bury Street, London EC3A 5AP
Dowgate Works, Douglas Road, Tonbridge

Printed in Great Britain by Brown Knight & Truscott Ltd. London

ISBN 0 85314 168 1

Contents

Contents

List of Illustrations

Acknowledgments

Acknowledgments are gladly made to the Radio Times Hulton Picture Library for permission to reprint Plate 1; to the Manchete Press Agency, Rio de Janeiro for Plates 2, 4, 6, 11, 12, 14, 15, 22, 26, 30; to the Camera Press, London for Plates 3, 5, 7, 9, 18, 20, 21, 27, 31, 32; to Varig Airlines for Plates 4, 6, 11, 12, 14, 15, 22, 26, 30; to Romano Cagnoni for Plate 28; to the United Press International for Plates 8, 10, 16, 17; to the *Economist* and *Jornal do Brasil,* Rio for Plate 13; to the Keystone Press, London for Plate 19; to Alberto Tamer for Plate 23; to *O Estado de São Paulo* for Plates 24, 25, 34; to Alfredo Rizzuti for Plates 24, 34; to the Associated Press for Plate 25; to Glyn Genin for Plate 29; to Robin Hanbury-Tenison for Plates 31, 32; and to *O Globo* for Plate 33.

I am also most grateful to the *Financial Times* for their consent to my use of material contained in articles written for them during 1966-69; to J. F. Trotter for drawing the maps and J. M. Shaftesley for preparing the Index; to Pat Gair for exemplary work in typing the manuscript and proof-reading; to Doris Woods and Irene Willis for editorial and secretarial assistance; to Xymena Wassilewska for timely aid from São Paulo; and, finally, to family and friends in England and Brazil who uncomplainingly helped in so many ways.

All translations in this text are the responsibility of the Author.

July 1972. G.H.C.

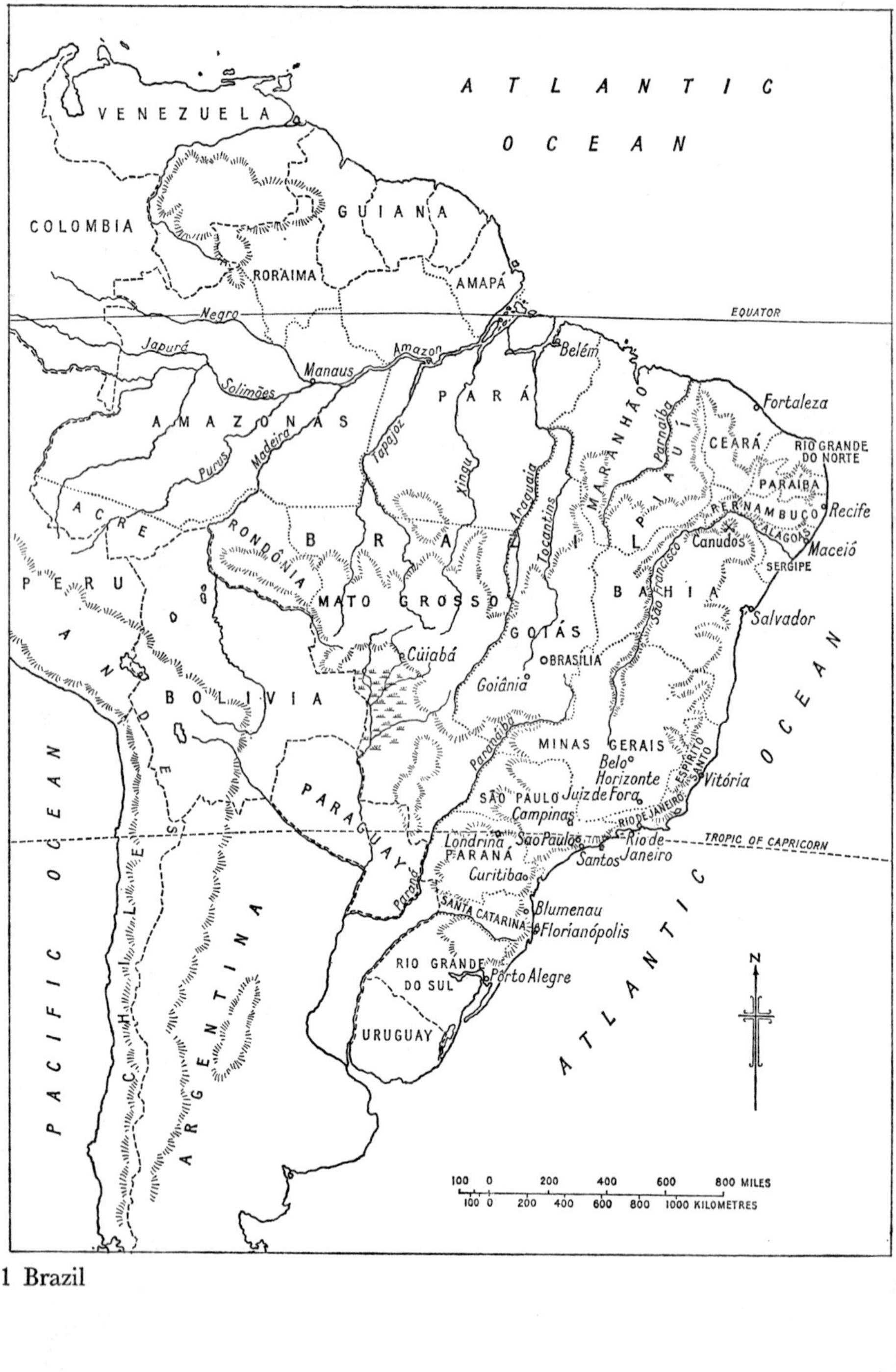
ATLANTIC OCEAN
VENEZUELA
COLOMBIA
GUIANA
RORAIMA
AMAPÁ
EQUATOR
Negro
Japurá
Amazon
Manaus
Solimões
Belém
PARÁ
Fortaleza
AMAZONAS
Purus
Madeira
Tapajoz
Xingu
Araguaia
Tocantins
MARANHÃO
Parnaíba
PIAUÍ
CEARÁ
RIO GRANDE DO NORTE
PARAÍBA
PERNAMBUCO
Recife
ALAGOAS
Maceió
SERGIPE
Canudos
ACRE
RONDÔNIA
BRAZIL
PERU
MATO GROSSO
BAHIA
São Francisco
Salvador
GOIÁS
Cuiabá
BRASILIA
Goiânia
ANDES
BOLIVIA
Paranaíba
MINAS GERAIS
Belo Horizonte
ESPÍRITO SANTO
Vitória
PARAGUAY
SÃO PAULO
Juiz de Fora
Campinas
RIO DE JANEIRO
Londrina
São Paulo
Rio de Janeiro
Santos
TROPIC OF CAPRICORN
PARANÁ
Curitiba
Paraná
SANTA CATARINA
Blumenau
Florianópolis
RIO GRANDE DO SUL
Pôrto Alegre
URUGUAY
PACIFIC OCEAN
CHILE
ARGENTINA
N
100 0 200 400 600 800 MILES
100 0 200 400 600 800 1000 KILOMETRES

1 Brazil

I

The People and the Land

> In tropical America there was formed a society agrarian in structure, slave-holding in its technique of economic exploitation and hybrid in composition, with an admixture of the Indian and later of the Negro.
>
> Gilberto Freyre, *The Masters and the Slaves*

The People

Not long after arrival, the visitor gives up trying to identify a typical Brazilian and settles down to enjoy the spectacle. Whether he is relaxing on the beaches of Rio de Janeiro, watching the display of the samba dancers at Carnival, or crossing the Viaduto do Chá, that human ant-hill in São Paulo, there is constant interest and entertainment for the eye. His senses are stimulated by the unending variations in colour, from white through all the intervening shades to jet-black, and by the multiplicity of European, African and Asiatic types, sometimes easily recognizable but often in the complex mixtures that are Brazil's speciality. Other Latin American countries provide something of the same sort of spectacle but none puts on the show that Brazil does; its melting-pot is apparently able to absorb any combination of elements and at times produces, as in the 'mulata'[1], an outstanding alloy.

The fusion of so many ingredients to create a nation, in which people at the various levels of society have a definite and on occasions even exuberant feeling for their country, is the achievement of Brazil. But it would be wrong to conclude, because of the apparent lack of friction in everyday racial contacts, that Brazil has reached the happy position of a country without race or colour problems.

The visitor to Brazil is usually conscious of the sharp conflicts, jarring attitudes and prejudices that these problems have engendered elsewhere, particularly in Anglo-Saxon countries. He may

[1] Mulata: a half-caste girl.

be hoping that at least in one country there is a success story, a multi-racial society that works. In Brazil he will find various aspects of race relations to encourage him: no official barriers have been erected there, in contrast with other countries; the constitution outlaws racial discrimination, the law forbids it in hotels and restaurants, prohibiting the mention of colour in police reports of offences and in applications for jobs.

In their daily life, Brazilians may seem far less conscious of race and colour than others, even 'colour-blind' in comparison with Anglo-Saxons, but it is too much to expect that they should have achieved a harmonious racial democracy. Brazilians have a keen awareness of colour. Many of them regard with satisfaction the trend towards whiteness, the 'bleaching' of the population, and the visitor may meet Brazilians (not necessarily pure whites themselves) who in outbursts against the backwardness of some aspects of Brazilian life, blame it on the 'prêtos' (blacks). Accustomed to behave with consideration in their daily contacts with those of a different race, Brazilians are nevertheless the heirs of problems inherited from the past. As was the case in other countries, Brazil for much of its history had a negro slave population that furnished the labour force for its principal economic activities, circumstances that left profound marks upon Brazilian society and contributed to its stratification. The national capacity for tolerance and permissiveness, together with a determined effort by socially conscious Brazilians who saw the dangers, prevented the emergence of a racial problem, but Brazilians could not avoid the creation of what currently appears as a class problem with a high colour correlation.

A French writer points to two levels in Brazilian culture: one archaic, at which living conditions are wretched, the other modern, and those at this level are improving their living standards rapidly. This division of the population into two levels of culture does not exactly correspond to its division between the various races, but as it happens, those with the darker skin are generally at the lower level.[1]

Thus, in Brazil, blackness in its association with economic and social inferiority is a barrier to advancement, as it is in those countries where the negro is in a minority and even in some where he forms a majority. Since so many things are lacking for the lower classes in Brazil, the negro experiences the same diffi-

[1] Jacques Lambert, *Os dois Brasis,* pp 30-1.

culties as the rest of the poor in finding a job, a roof or a school for his children. In employment, the advantages of the white or near-white skin—white is a suitably elastic term in Brazil—are evident; recruitment often exercises a tacit and at times more open discrimination in its favour and the negro finds himself at the lowest work levels, where he earns the minimum wage. Apart from the star negro football players, the great Pelé foremost amongst them, and from others in the entertainment world, the odds are against the negro breaking through the class barrier associated with his colour.

Will development, bringing with it, one hopes, a more open society and greater social mobility, increase the present meagre opportunities for the negro, indeed for the poor Brazilian generally, and equip him to play his part in progress? The question cannot be answered now. An expanding economy, so urgently needed, may create more opportunities for the negro and some negroes may take advantage of them. In the process of development, racial tensions, at present quiescent, may or may not emerge.

If the visitor nevertheless leaves Brazil convinced that it has achieved a better working relationship among the races than any other country with a multi-racial society, then much of the credit lies with the Portuguese. From the time of their discovery of Brazil at the beginning of the sixteenth century, they made up for the lack of Portuguese women during the colonization by miscegenation, first with the indigenous Indian women and later with the African women who came to Brazil with the consignments of negro slaves imported for work in the sugar plantations of the North-East and, during the late seventeenth and the eighteenth centuries, in the gold and diamond mines of Minas Gerais. In their home country, the Portuguese had been dominated from the eighth to the twelfth century by a dark-skinned race, the Moors, and were not prone to racial prejudice. Often said to prefer dark-skinned women, they were in any case impelled by circumstances to adopt a policy of miscegenation. Trading and exploration in Africa and Asia kept the little kingdom's limited manpower at full stretch, but the Portuguese offset this by the mobility and effectiveness of their navy and merchant fleet and by encouraging their settlers, who generally needed little encouragement, to breed a mestizo race that would populate the extensive territories overseas.

In Brazil, the Portuguese found none of the ready-made,

profitable trading opportunities that they had found in Asia, nor did they find any indigenous culture or civilization of significance, such as the Spanish conquistadores found long-established by the Incas in Peru and the Aztecs in Mexico. The native Indians were primitive nomads, living in scattered tribal communities dedicated to hunting, shooting (with bows and arrows) and fishing; a forest people, they cultivated few crops and had developed only a few rough implements. Although they were brave and used to warring amongst themselves, their opposition to colonization was soon overcome and the settlers found extremely ready partners among the Indian women, who regarded them as a superior race.

The Portuguese settlers were in fact a very 'mixed bunch'. With commitments in Asia and Africa, the government in Lisbon had few trained administrators to run the colony and govern the capitanias (captaincies or provinces) into which it was divided. The settlers came from the most varied sources. To some extent, the better class Portuguese families sent members out to the new colony, particularly to northern Brazil where a colonial aristocracy developed, but many of the settlers were adventurers, soldiers of fortune, exiles, Semitic new Christians, men of Moorish and Mozarabic origin, criminals and artisans intent on bettering themselves.

From early times in Brazilian history the three main elements in the racial mix began the process of fusion : the European with the indigenous Indian, the European with the African, the Indian with the African (the Asiatic was to arrive only in the twentieth century). The negro contribution to the process was not large in the early days of the colony. The Portuguese enslaved the Indians to form a labour force, sending expeditions into the interior to seize and bring them to work in the big estates on the coast that were from the outset a dominant feature of the colony's life and remained so. These expeditions, which in some respects fulfilled an exploring function—the Bandeirantes (Flag-bearers) from São Paulo were an example—spared none, also raiding the settlements organized by the Jesuit fathers and carrying off the Indians for sale in the slave-markets.

The Indians did not prove adaptable to many of the tasks required. The womenfolk, to whom the tribe allotted the tasks of agriculture and the home, formed a constructive element in the colonization process and enabled many settlers to raise families; but the men, useful in guiding parties exploring into the interior or in forming the defence forces to keep out pirates and invaders, were unsuited for the static life and regular tasks on the land, which they looked down on as women's work. The Portuguese therefore, who had had experience in the use of African slaves, turned to Africa for their labour supply when their wars with Holland ended and their sea lines of communication became clear.

The Portuguese drew the slave contingents that were to form the work force for the sugar plantations from a wide variety of African sources, including their mainland colonies and their island possessions. The various Bantu and Sudanese groups supplied most, but there were several other contributors. Some of the Sudanese negroes were Arabic-speaking Mohammedans, considered to have been superior in culture both to the Indians and indeed to the white colonists, many of whom were illiterate or had received little education. In an uprising in Bahia in 1835, these Moslem negroes startled the authorities by their use of written Arabic in organizing the rebellion.

The slave-ships brought these contingents to the slave-trade centres of Pernambuco, Bahia and Rio, from the seventeenth to the middle of the nineteenth century, in numbers not exactly known but reckoned in millions; it has been suggested that in 1850 there were some four million slaves in Brazil, accounting for more than half of the known population.[1] The Brazilian government made it virtually impossible to arrive at any accurate figure, when in 1890 it ordered the destruction of all the records and documents relating to slavery. With the passage of time, the slaves and their descendants were to be found in all the main regions of Brazil, including the southern states, where they worked on the coffee and cotton plantations of São Paulo and the farms and slaughter-houses of the far south; but the areas with which they came to be closely identified were the north-eastern states, particularly Bahia, where their cultural influence was strongest.

The negro proved to be better equipped physically to cope with the climate of tropical Brazil than either the indigenous Indian or the white man. Henry Bates, who in 1848 left his job at a Staffordshire brewery to become a naturalist in Amazônia, found that the Indians had a constitutional dislike of heat, being only cheerful on cool days when the rain was pouring down their

[1] Andrew Marshall, *Brazil,* p. 79.

naked backs, in contrast to the negro, the true child of tropical climates.[1] The latter proved more adaptable and vigorous than Indians or whites in the work on the plantations. Very quickly, therefore, the negro or negress became not only essential to the settler in the tasks of agrarian colonization, but also indispensable as the household servant and the nurse or companion of the master's children, exercising a considerable influence on the pattern of life and enriching the Brazilian vocabulary and diet. Bringing from Africa his own beliefs, the negro was to continue in Brazil his own fetishistic cults, which coexisted and at times blended with Roman Catholicism, making a characteristic contribution to Brazilian religious life.

Under this paternalistic system the negroes were often well-treated by their masters. The Portuguese indeed treated the negro much more humanely than did the English, French and Dutch on their colonial plantations in the Caribbean and the Americas, and spared the slaves harsh punishments that could have affected their working capacity.[2] It would have been surprising however if the institution of slavery had not given rise to friction between the white masters and the African slaves, and at times to revolt. Indeed the 'quilombos', backlands settlements of slaves who fled from the plantations or the mines, bore witness to this, an outstanding example being the confederation of settlements set up at Palmares in Alagoas, which lasted from 1630 to 1697, resisting repeated attacks but finally yielding to the superior forces of the colonists.[3]

In the course of time, the colony acquired a new status and then won its independence. Early in the nineteenth century the Napoleonic wars drove the Portuguese royal family to take refuge in Brazil. A Portuguese monarch, Dom João, ruled from Rio de Janeiro and in 1815 Brazil was declared a kingdom. When he returned to Lisbon in 1821, he left his son, Dom Pedro, behind as Regent, and a year later, as relations with the mother-country sharply deteriorated, Dom Pedro proclaimed the independence of Brazil and was crowned Emperor. Under him and especially during the long reign of his successor, Dom Pedro II, Brazil consolidated its newly won position and began to

[1] *The Naturalist on the River Amazons,* pp. 282-3.

[2] J. C. Garcia-Zamor, 'Social Mobility of Negroes in Brazil', written at the University of Texas at Austin, p. 2.

[3] José Honório Rodrigues, *The Brazilians,* p. 11.

1 Dom Pedro II, Emperor of Brazil 1840-89

2 Rio : the War Memorial, the Bay of Botafogo and the Sugar-loaf mountain

3 Rio : a 'favela' (shanty-town) covers a hillside

4 São Paulo : sky-scrapers mass in the heart of the city

develop a sense of nationhood. The country came however under increasing pressure from Europe and particularly from Britain to abolish slavery, one of the conditions that Britain made in agreeing to convince Portugal that it should recognize Brazilian independence. The problem of abolition became the foremost issue of Brazilian politics. In 1850 the Government banned the slave trade but only in 1871 took the next step: the freeing of all children born to slave mothers.

The final abolition of slavery in 1888, after years of nationwide debate and dissension, triggered off a national crisis that led to the abdication of the Emperor Dom Pedro II, the setting up of the Republic and the undermining of the economic framework built upon the availability of slave-labour. A further consequence was that immigration at last received a sharp impetus.

Until the nineteenth century Brazil had lived in comparative isolation from the outside world, its rulers in Lisbon relatively uninterested in granting foreigners facilities to settle in the colony. The vast territory drew its sparse population from three elements: its original inhabitants the Indians, the Portuguese settlers, whose numbers increased slowly with immigration, and the negro slaves working on the plantations. Then, in the first half of the century, there was a minor departure from the old immigration policy; the Portuguese-born rulers of Brazil encouraged a number of small-scale, planned settlements, made up of German and to a lesser extent Swiss and Italian immigrants. From these came the well-known Swiss colony at Nova Friburgo (taking its name from a Swiss canton) in the hills north-east of Rio, as well as small German ventures in Rio Grande do Sul and Santa Catarina.

The nineteenth century was one of large-scale European emigration to the Americas, especially to the U.S.A. and to Brazil's neighbour, Argentina. That mass movements of Europeans into Brazil only took place at a late stage was due in part to a failure to grant secure, liberal conditions of land tenure for people to settle in Brazil, a country of large estates and slave-labour. After the 1870s immigration and colonization policies were revised, but it was the abolition of slavery that created a demand for more hands and brought waves of European immigrants to settle on the fertile inland plateau and spur Brazil's drive to occupy its territory.

A new population was superimposed on an old one; a new Brazilian began slowly to emerge. Italians, Spaniards, Germans,

Poles and Japanese, to name the principal nationalities, settled in the Centre-South region, particularly in the state of São Paulo, which consistently subsidized the supply of immigrants to work as farm labourers and took a good half of the immigrants entering Brazil. To the southern states went many who were to be farm owners and operators, bringing to Brazil a potential rural middle class and an injection of new blood and skills that were to change the face of the country and transform its population. Of these the Italians, until 1930 when the flow of immigrants slackened, were the most numerous and congregated particularly in São Paulo and Rio Grande do Sul. The Germans settled mainly in Rio Grande and Santa Catarina where they showed considerable resistance to assimilation and set up well-organized communities with a strong Germanic outlook that influenced others living among them, even up to recent times; Gilbert Phelps, in a visit to these areas in the 1960s, found German-speaking negroes at Blumenau in Santa Catarina.[1] Among the new European groups were the Poles, who established themselves in Paraná.

This big movement was to include a particular contribution to the racial pattern. A fourth element arrived for the Brazilian melting-pot—the Japanese immigration, which was a twentieth century phenomenon.

From the day in 1908 when the S.S. Kasato Maru tied up at the port of Santos with some 800 farm-workers assigned to the coffee plantations of São Paulo, Japanese settlers moved into Brazil, over half of them coming from south-west Japan. Despite a ten year suspension of immigration during and after the Second World War, Japanese immigrants and their descendants came to number about 600,000, concentrated in the states of São Paulo and Paraná, but with small contingents in Rio de Janeiro, Mato Grosso and Amazônia.

In a nation that experienced a population explosion during the twentieth century, a colony of 600,000 might not be expected to have made a very significant impact, in comparison with the far more numerous settlements of Portuguese, Italian, Spanish and Germans, which provided the main European additions to the ingredients in the Brazilian melting-pot. However, the Japanese settlement, enjoying active support from the mother-country and being one of the most cohesive, exercised an influence out of proportion to its size, partly owing to its concentration in areas of

[1] *The Last Horizon*, p. 187.

great economic potential like São Paulo and Paraná, but also because the settlers proved to have farming skills and organizational abilities that Brazil desperately needed. Later, Japanese industry made in Brazil its largest overseas investment.

From the outset the Japanese immigrants took part in clearing the vast forests and opening up the fertile lands of São Paulo, helping to hasten the change from a coffee monoculture to a diversified agriculture. Bringing with them the traditions of work and intensive cultivation practised on small farms in Japan, the Japanese farmers in time undertook the cultivation of a wide range of crops, and the products of Japanese market-gardening, organized in cooperatives, revolutionized the diet of the Paulistas[1] who had hitherto eaten little more than rice, beans and beef. In northern Brazil the Japanese pioneered the growing of black pepper, centred at Tome-Açu near Belém, and along the Amazon they were successful in introducing the cultivation of jute from Pakistan. Innovators and organizers, late arrivals from a culture of characteristic features, the Japanese gave evidence of a slow assimilation into the Brazilian scene.

If the immigration of Europeans and Japanese was the outstanding phenomenon of the early twentieth century, the feature of the middle of the century was the population explosion.

Preliminary results of the 1970 Census, the first to be put on the computer, gave the total resident population as 93.2 m. and officials forecasted that in 1973 Brazil, already the eighth most populous country in the world, would reach the 100 m. mark. The yearly growth rate in the '60s had declined slightly to 2.8 per cent from the explosive rate of 3.0 per cent in the '50s. Life expectancy had increased greatly in the last decade; there had also been a substantial fall in the death-rate and even a small decline in the birth-rate. It was still however one of the highest population growth rates in the world.

Nobody looking at the vast expanses of Brazilian territory on the map would say that it was over-populated: with only 28 inhabitants per square mile, it was by European standards barely occupied. One could argue that there was no need to worry about a population explosion, since people would always be needed to take possession of, and develop, Brazil's empty spaces, which were almost embarrassingly extensive. Moreover, there was something attractive in the youthfulness of the population,

[1] Paulista: a native of the city or state of São Paulo.

the large number of children and young people everywhere, conveying an impression of a vigorous, expanding race that might make Brazil a genuine land of the future and not one of apparent promise that would never be fulfilled.

Closer study suggested however that there were grounds for anxiety over the headlong growth of population. In a country with large areas of poverty, suffering from a chronic shortage of capital, how were jobs to be created for the 1 m. new entrants a year into the labour market? How were schools, hospitals, homes, water supply and means of transportation to be provided, considering that in the '60s there was a serious shortage in these facilities because governments and public authorities had for long not been investing enough in them? If over half of the population were under 20, the burden on the working members of the population was obviously disproportionate; only a third of the population was directly contributing to the national wealth and the rest were merely consumers. Under these conditions, the pressure of rapidly increasing population would compel the government to devote a large part of investment solely to maintaining existing low standards, rather than to improving them.

There were still however many people in Brazil who were convinced that Brazil was far from having its optimum number of inhabitants, and that the population explosion did not matter; that the more Brazilians there were, the larger the domestic market would be. This was the view for quantity not quality. The new Brazil of the Centre-South was able to absorb a growing population but the situation in the other Brazil was distinctly uncomfortable. The population explosion was multiplying the human contingents in the North-East and was aggravating national problems that had been dragging on for decades, bringing in their wake an urban explosion of alarming proportions. The Census showed that in the '60s the urban population of Brazil for the first time exceeded the rural population, reflecting an exodus from the countryside that was also expressed in the growth of slums and shanty-towns, the 'mocambos' of Recife, the 'favelas' of Rio and the Cidade Livre of Brasília.

The Land

A sub-continent in size, with almost 3.3 m. square miles, Brazil is the fourth country in the world in contiguous land area (after the Soviet Union, Canada and China) and within South America has common frontiers with the three territories of the Guianas and all the other republics except for Chile and Ecuador. Measure the distances that Brazil covers from north to south and from east to west: they are 2,720 and 2,690 miles. It is more than twice as large as the present Western Europe and 35 times larger than the United Kingdom.

Among the countries that are in the 'major league' for size, Brazil distinguishes itself from the others as being genuinely tropical: the Equator lies across Northern Brazil and only 7 per cent of the country lies to the south of the Tropic of Capricorn and in the sub-tropical zone. With this tropical situation goes, basically, a tropical climate, which can be hot and humid, especially in the lowlands of the Amazon and in the long coastal belt. But there are appreciable variations and distinct varieties of climate may be identified; examples of these are the hot, dry climate of the north-eastern interior and the milder climate of the highlands, where the altitude brings coolness.

The topography of Brazil's western neighbours is dominated by the great chain of the Andes. Brazil has no mountains as formidable, but from the north of Bahia to beyond the northern border of Rio Grande do Sul runs the Serra, a high, rugged escarpment barring access from the coast to the interior. Drive from the port of Santos to São Paulo, up the Via Anchieta, named after a Jesuit missionary of the sixteenth century, or up the Estrada Velha ('old road') with its memories of the times of the Emperors, and you can imagine the sort of hostile country with which the early settlers had to contend. However, once the barrier of the Serra has been crossed, then the plateau of central and southern Brazil, stretching far inland, provides the fertile land and temperate climate that attracted the European settlers.

There are mountainous areas inland in Minas Gerais and Bahia, to the west in Mato Grosso and in the far north on the border with Venezuela, but the extensive lands of the interior are dominated by big rivers. In the south it is the Paraná, which joins with the River Paraguay outside Brazil's borders to form a river system comparable with the Mississippi-Missouri in the U.S.A. In the North-East are the rivers São Francisco and Parnaíba; in central Brazil, the Tocantins, the Araguaia (scene of Peter Fleming's *Brazilian Adventure*) and the Xingu; in northern Brazil, the Amazon and its tributaries, the basin of which, with its tropical rain-forests and grass-lands, covers a large part of the Brazilian land mass.

The Amazon basin does much more than this, however, because the great river system dominates half of South America. For David St. Clair the Amazon is 'not *a* river but a series of rivers that eventually meet to pour into the sea together', and are fed by the 'rains and melting snows from the Andes of Peru and Ecuador, from the melting snow of the Bolivian Altiplano, from rain storms breaking over the jungles of Colombia and Venezuela, from hidden springs and wells of the Guianas and from waters that have been collected in the vast unknown forests of Brazil.'[1] There is still controversy as to where in Peru its scource lies and some authorities identify one source that would make the river 4,500 miles long, the longest in the world, whereas the more conservative place the Amazon just behind the 4,000 miles of the Nile. The Amazon drains a total area of $2\frac{3}{4}$ m. square miles, and the larger of its one thousand-odd tributaries—the Madeira and the Purus for example—dwarf the rivers of other continents and delight the eye with their great sheets of water. Coming from widely different regions, they make startling contrasts when they meet. Leave Manaus, capital of the state of Amazonas, and as the plane turns beyond the city you see the meeting of the waters, the black River Negro, and the clearer, yellowish River Amazon (or Solimões as it is called locally) flowing along separately for a time between the same river banks and then slowly merging on their way to the sea.

According to one authority, the Amazon pours over $3\frac{1}{2}$ m. cubic feet of water into the Atlantic every second and carries with it more than 100 m. cubic feet of silt in 24 hours, its waters pushing out some 100 miles into the ocean.[2] There are about 30,000 miles of navigable water in the river basin and ocean-going ships of the Booth Line do the journey from the mouth of the river to Iquitos in Peru, about 2,300 miles away. The Spaniards take the credit for the first journey by Europeans down the great river.

In 1541 a Spanish expeditionary force left Quito in Ecuador, commanded by Gonzalo Pizarro, brother of Francisco Pizarro, the conqueror of Peru. Its purpose was to explore the interior to the east and search out its riches; in Ecuador, as in their other possessions in South America, the Spanish conquistadores had been listening eagerly to the current reports of the great wealth of 'El Dorado' and of a 'land of cinnamon', then a very valuable

[1] *The Mighty, Mighty Amazon,* p. 3.

[2] Andrew Marshall, *Brazil,* p. 18.

commodity in Europe. After the expedition had spent days on the road, it was joined by a party led by Francisco de Orellana, who had come up from the coast and was appointed by Pizarro as his lieutenant. The expedition ran into difficulties and became short of food. After discussion with Pizarro, Orellana left the rest of the party to search for supplies, taking to the river with a brigantine, some canoes and 60 men. Orellana and his men were never to rejoin the expedition. After travelling for several days and suffering starvation, cooking and eating the leather on their equipment, the soles of their shoes and any herbs they could find, they finally came to some friendly Indian settlements where they recovered their strength and morale. They decided that it was now impossible to go back upstream to the expedition and that the only thing to do was to carry on down the rivers until they could reach civilization again. After waiting for Orellana, Pizarro and his force struggled back to Quito in considerable distress.

The story of the adventures of Orellana's party was told by a Dominican friar who was with them, Gaspar de Carvajal.[1] They eventually came out into the River Marañon, so broad that they took it to be the fresh-water sea about which the Indians had told them. This was indeed the Amazon. From then on they suffered constant attacks from the Indians. In one of these Carvajal's head was pierced by an arrow and he lost an eye, while some of the soldiers died from poisoned arrows. Towards the end of the odyssey, which lasted eight months from the time when they left the expedition, they engaged in battle a force of Indians led by tall, white warrior women who, according to Carvajal, each did as much fighting as ten Indians and who ruled a region to the north of the river. These women lived in prosperous communities and were unmarried; when they wanted mates they secured them by making war on neighbouring tribes and bringing captives back to their villages for a season. Learning of this, the Spaniards found good reason to revive in the sixteenth century the legend of the Amazonian women of ancient Greece and they baptized the great river accordingly.

On returning to Spain, Orellana was made governor of the vast river territory that he had discovered, but his return to take possession was ill-fated and he died there. In due course the lands that he had claimed for Spain passed into the hands of Portugal, which through the opportunism of its men on the spot in

[1] See José Toribio Medina, *Discovery of the Amazon.*

Amazônia, succeeded in getting round the provisions of the Treaty of Tordesillas, the peace-making agreement by which Pope Alexander IV had carved up the new world between Spain and Portugal. Disregarding the restrictive boundary-line laid down in the Treaty and pushing Brazil's frontiers far out to the west, Portugal greatly expanded the territory of its new colony.

Orellana's journey was through the heart of a huge region on which man has made little impression over the centuries. Amazônia covers 42 per cent of Brazil's total area; today it is the least settled of all the regions. Its states of Amazonas, Pará and Acre, with the territories of Rondônia, Roraima and Amapá, have only a rarefied population, just over 3 per cent of the Brazilian total. It is part of the old, the other Brazil, in which two more regions are included. Of these, the North-East, which has 18 per cent of the national territory and covers the area from Maranhão to Bahia, contributes a population of 28.2 m., 30 per cent of the whole and a good deal of it concentrated in and around the cities. The Centre-West, consisting of the states of Mato Grosso and Goiás where the federal district of Brasília is situated, is a region of small if expanding population, only 5.8 per cent of the national total; geographically, this is the spring-board from which the attempt to organize a more effective occupation of Brazil's empty spaces is being made.

The new Brazil is the country of the Centre-South. With its focal point in the state of São Paulo, this region comprises the states of Minas Gerais, Espírito Santo, Rio de Janeiro, Guanabara (the city-state of Rio) and the states of the South-Paraná, Santa Catarina and the Rio Grande do Sul. All these states together account for only 18 per cent of the total land area, but in them live over 60 per cent of the total population.

The struggle to integrate

In the early 1960s forward-looking Brazilians were acutely conscious of the need not simply to change but to transform Brazil, to develop, integrate and modernize it. Aware of the degree of progress achieved in the developed countries of the West, they were all the more anxious to lift their own country out of its state of under-development and give it the position in the world appropriate to its sheer size and to its potential resources of men and materials, neglected for so long. The task was enormous and these thinking Brazilians had their own, at times differing, views of how it should be tackled. For the outside observer meanwhile, intrigued as to their chances of success, it was possible in 1960 to draw up a rough balance-sheet of some of the assets and liabilities that the country possessed in its struggle to integrate and develop.

Whatever its problems, Brazil possessed a firm territorial unity, thanks to the Portuguese and the Brazilians themselves, who had consolidated the national frontiers, prevented fragmentation and overcome infrequent outbreaks of separatism. No portion of the territory was currently anxious to be severed from the whole. The state of São Paulo had had ideas on these lines in the 1930s and had taken up arms to assert its right to the national leadership; Paulistas might complain now and then that their state was the locomotive pulling the 21 empty waggons of the federative republic but they seemed to have no intention of trying to uncouple them.

There were other assets, intangible in character. Brazilians could point to a consciousness of national identity and to a national pride. They spoke a common language, Portuguese, used uniformly throughout Brazil, more musical in its Brazilian accent and more extensive in its vocabulary than the language of the mother-country. Also, religion was on the whole a unifying factor. Though by no means a religious people, Brazilians broadly considered themselves as Roman Catholics. Catholicism, praised by Freyre as 'the cement of our unity' was a rallying point for the colony and in due course became the official religion.

In 1960, three main institutions were capable of playing a leading role in a process of integration and development, or of assisting it. This ability existed in the national government to the extent that it exercised an effective national leadership and was prepared to give direction and support to the process. It existed in the armed forces, through the experience gained by their career officers and NCOs in serving in the various regions of the country, and through their capacity to transport people and equipment throughout the national territory and to communicate over long distances. Finally, it was present in the Church. This had come to Brazil with the early settlers, as had the religious orders, particularly the Jesuits, who played an important role in education in the first 200 years of the colonial period.

The Church did not apparently acquire a position of great strength. 'Seen in historical perspective', writes E. de Kadt, 'the Catholic church in Brazil has never been a particularly powerful institution, certainly not when compared with most other Latin American countries, where a strong and above all rich church was entrenched near the top of the colonial structure of domination'.[1] Separated from the state in 1890, the Church was potentially able, through its power of communication and the clergy's access to all classes of society, to exercise influence on a nation-wide scale and to assist the process of national integration.

The process, however, required a dynamic centre to initiate and disseminate change, and this centre was the city and state of São Paulo. To this temperate and fertile area with its characteristic red earth, lying 2,600 feet above sea level, came in the late nineteenth and early twentieth century the waves of Italians, Spanish, Levantines and Japanese, attracted by a prosperity first derived from coffee production and later from the broad industrial and agricultural development that transformed the state. The Italians were the principal economic force in this immigration; the late Count Matarazzo was one example of an immigrant who arrived with nothing, started work as a barrow-boy selling oranges and went on to build an enterprise that is today one of the largest privately-owned concerns in Brazil. Commercial empires were built and fortunes were made in the fierce competition to get on in the world. The traders from the Levant were as conscious of status as the rest. Arriving as mere 'Turks', they would graduate to 'Syrians' when their business prospered, finally presenting themselves in society as 'Lebanese' when they hit the jackpot.

São Paulo also became the Mecca for migrants from the less-developed regions of Brazil, particularly from the impoverished North-East, where workers left harsh living conditions to look for jobs in São Paulo's factories and farms. Rated as the fastest growing, eighth largest city in the world—and possessing a considerable middle class—São Paulo saw its population in the municipal area grow from 1.3 m. in 1940 to over 3.8 m. in 1960 with many more in Greater São Paulo, which included such industrial areas as the 'ABC' towns of Santo André, São Bernardo and São Cayetano. The rapid growth engendered serious problems of congestion and pollution, and the public services wilted under the strains of trying to meet the needs of a population that was expanding much too quickly.

[1] *Catholic Radicals in Brazil,* London, Oxford University Press (Royal Institute of International Affairs), 1970, p. 51.

By the year 1960, São Paulo was firmly established as the commercial and industrial capital of the new Brazil, which looked to Paulista enterprise to lead the nation's development. Half of Brazil's industrial capacity lay in greater São Paulo and a little under half of its agricultural production came from São Paulo state, with coffee, cotton, sugar, rice and maize the principal crops.

On the industrial side, motor vehicles, electrical goods, chemicals, textiles, telecommunications equipment and metal-working plants formed the backbone of Paulista manufacturing industry, which was supported by a well-developed banking network and a labour force numbering over a million. Many of the big international companies were strongly represented, particularly in the motor vehicle industry which included large plants of Volkswagen, Mercedes Benz, General Motors and Ford, as well as many smaller factories turning out vehicle parts. In this industry and others, São Paulo accumulated the new techniques and expertise coming from abroad and provided a channel for them to be disseminated to the rest of the country. The state of São Paulo became the largest electric-power producer in Brazil and in Santos possessed the major port of Brazil serving a large hinterland.

With its industry complemented by technical institutions and training and educational facilities in advance of the rest of Brazil, São Paulo was in a position to influence the course of events in the remainder of the country. The level of activity at this industrial and commercial centre of gravity largely determined the shape of things elsewhere. Moreover, federal schemes to develop more backward regions such as the North-East and Amazônia, needed co-operation from Paulista businessmen and industrialists for their success. In fact, there was a danger of the excessive concentration of activity in São Paulo and of the rest of the country becoming tributary to it.

The progress manifested in São Paulo's agricultural and industrial development was to spread in the twentieth century to the other states of the Centre-South, where it was much less uniform. Minas Gerais for example, despite its potential, remained traditional and conservative. The states of Rio de Janeiro and Espírito Santo were slow to advance and Santa Catarina had less progress to show than one might have expected. Large and small pockets of the archaic persisted in the unpredictable manner typical of Brazil, but the general movement forward was unmistakable and in some areas rapid. In the national struggle to integrate, São Paulo was without doubt a principal asset.

What was there on the other side of the balance-sheet in 1960? We shall discuss two main liabilities.

In relation to Brazilian aspirations to become a modern, progressive country, the first liability lay in education where there were glaring contrasts between the new and the old Brazil. The Census figures for the population over 15 years old showed that the percentage of illiterates (people unable to read or write a simple message) dropped from 51 per cent in 1950 to 39 per cent in 1960. This marked the progress made, regionally speaking, in the Centre-South and nationally in the cities. In the rural areas where the school, if there was one, was often miles away from the home and where the family often needed the youth's labour at an early age, the figures were relatively much less favourable. The North-East had half the illiterates in the whole country and, because of the population explosion, their number in the North-East had grown from 4.9 m. in 1920 to 5.2 m. in 1960.[1]

Nationally, the states and municipalities bore the responsibility for primary education and the wealthier states, such as São Paulo, were always able to make a bigger relative effort than the poorer states, despite federal financial help to the latter. Thus, the tendency was for the richer states, thanks to their higher levels and reserves of better trained people, to advance faster and for the poorer ones to fall farther behind.

During the nineteenth century and indeed for part of the twentieth century, education was for the elite, few in numbers, in whose hands power was concentrated and who were often able to complete their education abroad, in Portugal, France, England or the U.S.A. Until 1920 there were no Brazilian universities. In the colonial times, the Portuguese had taken the view that anyone in Brazil needing higher education should be sent to the universities of Lisbon or Coimbra, and this attitude persisted under the Emperors and even under the Republic. It was an era of education for status, with its goal the title of 'doutor', still used to indicate social superiority. Even after the revolution of 1930, the process of making education available to the masses and of introducing a genuine universal type education to fit the needs

[1] Rubens Vaz da Costa, 'O crescimento demográfico do Nordeste e o desenvolvimento nacional', Fortaleza, 1970, p. 15.

of a developing society, was slow and held back Brazil's advance. Thus, throughout a period when the population explosion greatly increased the numbers of young people, progress, though ultimately accelerated, was not enough to make up for past neglect; in 1950 only between 6 and 7 per cent and in 1960 just over 11 per cent of those eligible went to secondary school.

Educational experts agreed that the university system required a drastic overhaul. The 29 universities, the majority of which were in the new Brazil, were run, in roughly equal proportions, by the federal or state governments, or by private authorities, mainly religious orders; overall supervision was exercised by the Ministry of Education and federal funds were supplied on a substantial scale. Indeed, money was not the basic difficulty; the real problem lay in the poor return on the existing investment.

University education was free of charge, though many of the students came from the upper and middle classes and would be well able to contribute to the expenses. In 1960 under 2 per cent of the population in the corresponding age group actually obtained admission to a university and there were serious imbalances and deficiencies in the facilities and staff available to teach students in the various faculties. With the exception of states such as São Paulo, the distribution of courses in the universities was largely divorced from the demands of the labour market and of the process of development. Half of the graduates in any one year were in law and philosophy; economics, sociology and dentistry also figured very highly, but engineers, scientists and agronomists were turned out only in very meagre numbers. The equipment and facilities for these studies were correspondingly inadequate.

In the educational sector a massive effort was needed to raise the standards in the new Brazil; in the other Brazil marked by the colonial tradition and unaffected by the processes that were transforming the Centre-South, such an effort was required on an extraordinary scale. Here, there were strong barriers to overcome, above all in the mentality of the ruling classes and of the people. In the great expanse of these territories, many communities of the interior had been living in relative isolation, often having few links with the outside world. A rural way of life had persisted, based on a primitive agriculture and a paternalistic form of organization dependent on the personal relationship between the landowner and the peasant, on an unchanging two-class society dominated by the 'colonels' (landowners so named because they held honorary rank in the state militia).

A second, main liability in the aspiration to become a modern, progressive country lay in transport and communications.

The sub-continental size of the country, its 4,500 mile coastline, big rivers and great distances separating centres of population (with São Paulo 1,300 and 1,500 miles, as the crow flies, from the north-eastern and northern cities of Recife and Belém), all placed a premium on the building up of an adequate transport and communications system. To carry out this task was one of the big long-term planning and engineering challenges of all time. As in the twentieth century the process of development began to get under way, the dimensions of the task became more apparent. Farming areas required effective links with the growing cities and with export centres, mining zones needed transport facilities to move minerals to processing plants or the ports, and industry began to realize the necessity of developing markets in the interior.

Sea and river, road and rail transport required development. The Brazilians did not inherit the sea-faring traditions of the Portuguese and the road was the principal instrument used in the attempt to open up Brazil in the twentieth century. Governments periodically tried to grapple with the overall problem but there was insufficient investment to provide the facilities required on the necessary scale, or to maintain the productivity of the railways, the ports and the merchant marine. Therefore, the infrastructure needed to overcome the obstacles of distance was lacking; the country remained an 'archipelago of islands' with deficient inter-communication. Only the advent of air transport, from the 1930s onwards, brought to those who could afford it the facility of travel that Europeans and Americans took for granted.

In 1960, worse and more irritating deficiencies were to be found in telecommunications, which in large regions of the country were non-existent. For the Brazilian businessman trying to keep in touch with his suppliers and customers, for the North-easterner wanting to call his relations in the South, for the ordinary citizen going about his everyday activities, communication was a real source of frustration.

Some services worked efficiently. There were always well-run international cable companies, such as the Western Telegraph Company. But a real cause for exasperation lay in the deficiencies of the telephone system, totally inadequate to meet the needs of development and requiring a sustained effort of investment in equipment and staff to bring it up to a reasonable level.

Both during the Second World War and for many years after, the telephone companies in Brazil, whether foreign, municipal or private, came under the constant pressures of chronic inflation, and, frequently, the refusal of the authorities to grant the tariff increases that would have enabled the companies to pay their way and generate funds for expansion.

Under these conditions, the telephone services went steadily downhill in the very years when Brazil was undergoing a process of rapid industrialization, together with a high population growth rate. In the early '60s Brazil had less than two telephones per 100 inhabitants, compared with a reported world average of six, to say nothing of nearly 19 in Britain and 48 in the U.S.A. Even in the cities, telephones were few and only too liable to go out of action when there was a heavy fall of rain. In Rio, when the 'bankers' of Brazil's numbers game with animals, the 'jôgo de bicho', were operating over the telephone network, one might just as well give up trying to get a line.

In another key sector of communication, the domestic postal service, such post boxes as existed were dignified, archaic iron contraptions, relics from the days of the Empire, into which nobody was so rash as to drop a letter; business and industry still turned to a private enterprise mail-bag system, the indispensable 'malote' to get the mail delivered. There was a crying lack of facilities for a country needing to encourage the spread of new ideas and techniques.

In the struggle to integrate, develop and modernize, Brazil suffered from growing pains that were also expressed in the vicissitudes of its political life. The revolution of 1930 and the political crises of the 1950s and 1960s were symptoms of its difficulties in solving its problems. A country in ferment was to witness the events of 1964, marking one of the sharpest changes of course in this century.

2 The Vargas Era and the Experiment in Democracy

The Vargas era: 1930-45

A new era in Brazilian politics, heralding more rapid economic and social change, began in 1930 when the government of President Washington Luís, the last of the 'old Republic', fell to the onslaught of a revolution headed by Getúlio Vargas, who directly or indirectly was to exercise a major influence on the course of Brazilian politics for over three decades.

Revolution was in the air among the South American republics, which were feeling the sharp impact of the economic crisis that had begun with the stock-market crash on Wall Street. In Brazil, the Republic, set up in 1889 on the abdication of the Emperor, had for some time been suffering a process of agitation, including a good half-dozen uprisings since 1922, and its institutions, dominated by an old, corrupt oligarchy, were beginning to look distinctly shaky. The revolt of 1930 was sparked by resentment at the growing political and economic power of the fast-developing state of São Paulo, with President Luís, himself a Paulista, preparing to install another one in the Presidency, in accordance with the election results but contrary to the traditional electoral alliance with the Mineiros[1], who had been expecting to supply the next President. It was supported by the political and economic interests of Minas Gerais and Rio Grande do Sul (Vargas' home state), by senior army officers anxious for reform and by nationalistic younger officers known as the 'Tenentes' (Lieutenants). Many of the latter had taken part in the risings of the '20s and they aspired to modernize and reorganize the national life and institutions, believing that this should be done 'by a totally uncompromised cadre of non-political technocrats with an unswerving sense of national mission'.[2] Some of these men, by then senior officers, were to play a prominent role in the events of the '50s and '60s.

[1] Mineiro : a native of the state of Minas Gerais.

[2] T. E. S. Skidmore, *Politics in Brazil,* p. 10.

5 President
Getúlio Vargas,
in his later years

6 President
Juscelino Kubitschek

7 January 1961, the Presidential inauguration at Brasília: President-elect Jânio Quadros chats with President Kubitschek. On the left Vice-President João Goulart.

8 August 1961: Goulart in Paris, returning to Brazil to assume the Presidency

9 Carlos Lacerda

10 General Castello Branco, as Army Chief of Staff

11 Castello talks with a top Church leader

12 Roberto de Oliveira Campos

The desire for political change that motivated the revolt of 1930 was reinforced by the effects of the world depression, which awoke Brazil to the realities of its vulnerable position as an under-developed country with a colonial-type economy dependent on exports of raw materials and imports of manufactures. The collapse of prices for its exports, particularly of coffee, and a financial crisis at home made the country ready for new management. A Macchiavelli among politicians, Vargas assumed the leadership of the forces that made the revolution, and kept himself in power for the next 15 years.

He was born of a cattle-ranching family in Rio Grande do Sul and displayed early in local state politics a prudence and discretion that enabled him to move steadily up the ladder, to the state governorship and in due course to the position of candidate in the 1930 Presidential elections. Enigmatic and careful not to commit himself, but affable and tolerant of others, not making enemies if he could possibly avoid it, he wanted power and was prepared to exercise patience and to compromise in order to win and keep it.

Coming from a prosperous middle-class background, he had the political ability to interpret the feelings of the humblest Brazilians and to identify himself with their thoughts and aspirations. As a political leader, he maintained his power by shrewdness and outmanoeuvring his opponents without any complete party organization behind him nor a well-defined ideology, but with a capacity to get the public to blame his aides and not him when things went wrong. During the 15 years in which he ruled, for much of the time with absolute power, Brazilian society moved at an increasing tempo from a rural society based on the landowner and the big estate producing for export, to an urbanizing society with growing middle and working classes and with an expanding industry to meet the demands of the domestic market. Vargas took good note of the changing times and moved with them.

In 1932, as head of the provisional government, he put down a revolt by the Paulistas, who distrusted his intentions, and two years later became President, having supervised the approval of a new constitution under which elections were supposed to be held later to choose his successor. Meanwhile, the political movements typical of the Europe of that time began to organize and bid for power in Brazil: the Communists, led by the former revolutionary Tenente, Luís Carlos Prestes, a romantic figure who had led a rebel column in the '20s on a 'long march' through the interior, and the Fascists, in the green-shirted Brazilian version named 'Integralism'. In 1935 Vargas suppressed Communist uprisings in the North-East and Rio de Janeiro, where the insurgents murdered army officers and men in their barracks, an event that in future years was to be regularly recalled on the day of its anniversary.

As the end of his term as President began to approach in 1938 and electioneering began for the appointment of his successor, Vargas took shrewd advantage of threats, real or stage-managed (including a forged 'Communist action' plan), from the Communist and Fascist movements and moved to fulfil his own authoritarian ambitions. With the support of some senior officers of the armed forces and the acquiescence of others, he closed Congress and sent the deputies home. Then he cancelled the elections and set up the 'Estado Nôvo' (new state), a corporate Fascist-type regime, similar to contemporary Italian and Portuguese models though milder in form, under which he ruled virtually as a dictator until 1945.

The period of Vargas' authoritarian rule saw him working to strengthen the central government at the expense of the states and stepping up his efforts to win working-class support, which he had consistently cultivated. His creation of a Ministry of Labour, Industry and Commerce in 1930, then of trade unions tied to it and of labour courts to protect the employee, as well as the setting up of elaborate social security schemes, were aimed to benefit a class that had been politically and socially neglected, and of which Vargas was to become the idol. The volume of money in the hands of the bodies administering these schemes greatly increased the powers of political patronage and leverage available to the regime.

The Second World War provided opportunities for Vargas to give further impetus to Brazil's industrialization. The Americans needed facilities for bases in North Brazil; these were granted and assisted the movement of troops and supplies to North Africa. In return, Vargas obtained American loans for setting up the first integrated steel plant at Volta Redonda. Public investment in the development of minerals and in land reclamation was increased, and private investors were encouraged to put money into industry to strengthen the domestic market. The cities and the urban middle classes grew apace.

As an authoritarian ruler Vargas began by favouring the Axis powers in the Second World War, but he yielded to the requirements of Pan-American solidarity and to public opinion in favour of the Allies, agreeing to the sending of an expeditionary force to Italy to fight by their side. Realizing that his type of regime could hardly outlive the war, he saw the need to modify the authoritarian style of his government. With an eye to his own political future, he set up a Brazilian Labour Party (Partido Trabalhista Brasileiro or PTB) based on the government-sponsored trade unions, and a party of the elite broadly representing the rural landowners and the new industrialists, the Social Democratic Party (Partido Social Democrático or PSD); the two in Vargas' concept were to work together.

Vargas could not resist the pressures in 1945 to hold elections and introduce the democratic processes, but when he began to meddle with the electoral regulations and to secure his brother's appointment as police chief of the federal capital, the army, its suspicions aroused, stepped in to demand his resignation. The two leading generals, Góes Monteiro and Dutra, who had supported the coup d'état of 1937, were now most active in securing Vargas' departure.

The experimental democracy 1945-64

The period that began late in 1945, with Vargas' temporary exit from the political limelight, and ended with the deposition of President Goulart in 1964, was one of recurrent crises, imposing burdens on the political framework that it finally proved unable to bear. Of the five elected Presidents two succeeded in completing their terms of office; one committed suicide, one resigned after seven months in office and the third was deposed. There were various military interventions in the course of political events, culminating in the revolt of March 31st, 1964.

National elections, the first since 1934, took place in December 1945, with the anti-Vargas elements mainly grouped in the National Democratic Union (União Democrática Nacional or UDN), a party formed in 1945 from the urban middle classes. The Communist party, partially recovered from the stigma of its disastrous coup in 1935, also took part in the elections, competing with the three main parties and winning a number of seats in Congress[1]; it emerged as the fourth most powerful party in Brazil and the strongest Communist party in Latin America,

[1] Ibid, pp. 61-2.

with particular appeal to youth. Vargas was elected a senator for the PSD and retired to his farm near the Argentine border. The new President, elected on the basis of a PSD/PTB alliance was General Dutra, Vargas' former War Minister.

General Dutra's government completed its term without being seriously threatened. Early in his regime, a new constitution, with guarantees of free elections and civil liberties, was passed by Congress meeting as a constituent assembly. The new President however cracked down on the Left, obtaining a court decision to suppress the Communist Party whose leader, Luís Carlos Prestes, had identified it with the Soviet Union, saying that in the event of war between the latter and Brazil, the party would fight for the Soviet Union.

President Dutra was a moderate who slept with a copy of the constitution on his bedside table and his government was unspectacular. In economic policy he moved cautiously but witnessed the rapid running down of the exchange reserves accumulated during the war. A tentative effort was made to plan public investments on a long-term basis and to promote development through the 'Salte' plan, based on investment in health, food supply, transport and power. In the absence of serious political disturbances, some satisfactory rates of economic growth were registered, especially in industry. Brazil was quiet, even more so after Dutra had closed the casinos. Meanwhile, however, Vargas had been actively preparing his return to power and in the 1950 elections, with the aid of some carefully chosen allies, he was swept back into office with 49 per cent of the votes.

The return of the old dictator, now in democratic guise, found Vargas more tired and reserved, less able to manipulate and control the political forces of his time. His personal prestige and popularity amongst the people remained but he faced stronger political opposition, chiefly from the UDN, while the military, who had uneasily watched him regain power by constitutional means, were now viewing his moves with evident distrust.

Vargas in his new, democratic phase turned once more to the policy of building up industry, but he now gave greater attention to overcoming the deficiencies in transport, power and the other basic facilities essential to economic growth. Here he co-operated with the U.S.A. and followed the recommendations of a joint Brazil-United States Commission in setting up the National Bank for Economic Development (BNDE), which was to play an important part in directing public money into investments in the infrastructure. Aiming to give strong central direction to the economy, Vargas took a significant, nationalist step in establishing Petrobrás, a state-controlled company with a monopoly in oil exploration and production. His wish to move decisively towards greater economic independence was thwarted by the emergence of balance-of-payments difficulties, and his ambitions in the field of development met with tough inflationary problems. His stabilization programme failed to beat inflation, setting a precedent that later administrations were to follow.

The regime met with serious economic obstacles, but it was Vargas' ignorance of what was going on behind his back, his failure to control corruption and discipline his subordinates that brought about his end. In August 1954, members of his personal bodyguard, without the President's knowledge, hired a gunman to assassinate one of the regime's most vigorous and persistent critics, the journalist Carlos Lacerda, but the killer failed, slightly wounding Lacerda and killing his escort, an Air Force major. The incident destroyed the President's authority and, in an atmosphere of great tension, the armed forces once more stepped in to demand his resignation. This time Vargas met their ultimatum with his suicide, leaving a dramatic letter defending his political career and attacking his enemies. Throughout the country, there was anger and grief amongst his followers.

Vargas' death, presented by his supporters as martyrdom, created bitter hostility between them and his opponents. In an atmosphere of tension the Vice-President, Café Filho, set up a caretaker government and went ahead with the programme of national elections. The victory went to Juscelino Kubitschek of the PSD and João Goulart, Chairman of the PTB, both connected with the Vargas forces and winning a hard-fought contest, in which the PSD/PTB coalition again defeated their UDN rivals. Kubitschek received under 36 per cent of the votes and became President-elect with a minority vote; his running-mate Goulart won more support from the voters but was considered by some, including elements of the military, to be a highly undesirable choice because of his left-wing views and easy relations with the Communists.

A chorus of dissatisfaction over the election results was led by the anti-Vargas spokesman, Carlos Lacerda, who from his newspaper desk headed a movement to get the military to stop the two men from taking office. Café Filho suffered a heart attack and was replaced by the speaker of the Chamber of Deputies, Carlos Luz, as acting President. Meanwhile General Lott, Minister of War under Café Filho and a key figure in these events, had been struggling to keep the army out of politics and ensure respect for legality, He lost his post under Luz, whose intentions he distrusted. With support from like-minded officers he acted, mobilizing the Rio garrison in a coup to guarantee the presidential succession in accordance with the election results. Yet another acting President was installed and a state of siege was maintained until the inauguration of President Kubitschek in January 1956.

With this overture of confusion, it was surprising that President Kubitschek finished his term of office without political turmoil. Although he came to the Presidency as a prominent Mineiro politician, his origins were quite humble—his widowed mother was a school teacher whose Czech forbears came to Minas Gerais early in the nineteenth century. The young Juscelino put himself through eight years of medical school by working as a telegraph operator at night. Having qualified as a surgeon, he saw service at the front in 1932 with the Vargas forces fighting against the rebellion of the Paulistas and made personal contacts that proved invaluable in launching him on a political career. He quickly worked his way up through the local Vargas political machine in Minas, to become mayor of Belo Horizonte in 1940 and then state governor, in which position he made his mark in a dynamic growth policy, concentrating on road-building and electric power development, with the aim of attracting new industry and development to this stronghold of conservative landowners and the traditional Minas families.

Kubitschek was a self-made man and he brought to the Presidency an infectious confidence (his critics would add: and a streak of irresponsibility). If he kept the peace during his term, it was thanks to his political skill in managing Congress, particularly in avoiding direct clashes with his opponents, and to his pursuit of policies in which there was something for everybody and patronage was liberally used to reward friends and buy off opposition. He showed particular skill in manipulation of the old party political machines, tolerating their corruption and putting them to work. Not an outstanding speaker, he nevertheless had some talents of the demagogue and great ability to communicate and gain popularity with the people. Conscious of the balance of forces in Brazilian politics, he was careful to satisfy the needs of the armed forces for higher pay and new equipment and to stick to programmes that would command a good measure of support from the officer corps.

In foreign affairs, he cultivated relations with the U.S.A., undertaking a considerable public relations effort to persuade the American government and public opinion to interest themselves in his programme. He did, however, look further than exclusively Brazilian interests and, conscious of the gross underdevelopment and dire poverty of much of Latin America, he made imaginative proposals for a common effort to promote Latin American development, the 'Operation Pan-America', which appealed to many in the region and eventually found a more dynamic response in the establishment of the Alliance for Progress—when the crisis in relations with Castro's Cuba convinced the Americans that something more must be done in hemispheric co-operation.

At home, Kubitschek succeeded in mobilizing popular support and even enthusiasm by adopting expansionist policies based on an all-out development programme consisting of 30 individual targets, with the slogan 'Fifty years progress in five'. In his election campaign, he had already broadly outlined a national development plan, in which private enterprise, with the guidance and encouragement of the government and assistance from foreign capital, would play a major role in developing Brazil's resources and improving living standards. Much of the groundwork for the plan was already to hand, in the work carried out by a team of economists drawn from the National Bank for Economic Development and the U.N. Economic Commission for Latin America.

Creating his own 'brains trust' of technocrats, Kubitschek on taking office spelled out his plan in the Target Programme (Programa de Metas) of specific goals to be achieved in power, transport, food supply, basic industries and technical education, placing the supervision of the programme under a council whose establishment for the first time envisaged development planning on a lasting basis. The government encouraged the private sector by offering liberal credit and an expanding domestic market, setting ambitious targets for production of, for example: metals, cement, paper, rubber, capital goods and above all motor vehicles, which prompted the expansion or introduction of factories by the big international companies, both W. German and American, bringing an important dynamic factor into Brazilian industry.

The Programme also involved the stepping up of public investment in various sectors.

The achievements were impressive—power generation, oil production, refinery capacity, road-building, iron and steel production all scored considerable gains and in the private sector electrical goods, motor vehicles and fertilizers, to name a few, made striking advances. It was a period of industrial boom—industrial production went up by around 80 per cent during the Kubitschek administration, but in contrast it did relatively little in important sectors like general education and agriculture, although it increased storage facilities and the use of tractors. The whole policy marked a significant shift in the attitude to foreign capital, since the regime contracted large foreign loans and gave strong encouragement to private foreign interests, in the process greatly increasing the share of international companies in Brazilian industry. The Programme could not, however, be carried out without extensive borrowing at home and abroad, and the volume of government spending kept the presses busy printing money and stoked the fires of inflation.

President Kubitschek restlessly turned his attention to other problems. A man of vision, intent on waking Brazilians up to the tasks of doing something with their country, he was very reluctant to consider the cost of things—very low on arithmetic, he was a big spender in a poor country. He turned to the troubles of the other Brazil. A first step was taken in facing the problems of developing the impoverished North-East. Above all, Kubitschek, a man from a small town (Diamantina, an old diamond mining centre) in the interior of Minas, acted to change the attitudes of Brazilians by encouraging the movement away from the coast and into the interior. With feverish energy he set about the building of a new federal capital, 600 miles inland, on the bare plateau of eastern Goiás, at Brasília. The determination and drive put into the work of completing this project, which had remained on paper for so many decades, was a stimulus to national pride, but the building of Brasília was carried out at a speed and cost that paved the way for the rampant inflation that threatened to devour Brazil in the '60s. It was this headlong use of the scarce resources of a poor country, in the rush to finish the new capital during the Kubitschek administration, that would lead some Brazilians to say of this, the spending aspect of the Kubitschek regime: 'Foi uma loucura' ('It was madness').

Inflation had continued to be a serious problem, reaching 25 per cent in the first year of the Kubitschek administration. In 1958, the financial brains of the regime brought out a stabilization programme to check the rapid rate of price increases, but political hostility to anti-inflationary measures and the President's refusal to back the programme wholeheartedly led to its abandonment and the departure of the men that had prepared it. In a nationalist gesture, from which he extracted the maximum benefit, President Kubitschek broke off relations with the International Monetary Fund in Washington, which had been advising the Brazilian authorities on the programme's implementation.

The confidence generated among Brazilians during the exciting Kubitschek years wilted under the impact of the political crises of the '60s.

It was on a reform ticket that Jânio Quadros, who had been a successful governor of São Paulo, came to the Presidency in 1961, after a massive popular vote and an election campaign in which his symbol had been a broom to sweep corruption out of government and impose austerity in the administration of public affairs. Many of the voters, worried at the growth of inflation, hoped that Quadros would show the same capacity for choosing rational financial policies and sensible administrators that he had shown in running São Paulo. Without any Vargas ties, a political outsider and independent, who made little effort to cultivate party support, Quadros won the election nominally as the UDN candidate, while João Goulart, who had not in fact been his running-mate, once more won the Vice-Presidency.

Quadros had charisma, a great ability to communicate with the common man, who saw in him a leader unconnected with the 'establishment'—the politicians and the ruling classes who had always controlled everything. In this talent for reaching the people, which Quadros fostered by his highly informal dress and untidy appearance, he had some of the qualities of Vargas.

Quadros' first action as President was to broadcast to the nation a vehement criticism of the financial situation inherited from the Kubitschek administration, which he called terrible. The country had been brought to the brink of financial collapse; it was faced with huge budget and balance-of-payments deficits and with vastly increased internal and foreign debts, imposing crippling repayment obligations to be met in 1961 and the years ahead, Quadros said. Too much money had been spent with too much publicity. The future had been heavily mortgaged and the situation could only be restored by sacrifice and a patient effort to raise the money, dollar by dollar and cruzeiro by cruzeiro. It was a black picture, but Quadros said that he was not exaggerating.

The new President lost no time in making a broad sweep with the new broom. He set up over 30 investigating committees to look into alleged graft and corruption in government agencies under the previous administration. Numerous targets were selected, including the 'Novacap' (the agency that had built Brasília), the Amazonian development superintendency SPVEA, whose administration and financial management had recently aroused severe criticism and, above all, the social security institutes. President Kubitschek had given Vice-President Goulart control of labour and social welfare as part of the political bargain and the institutes' payrolls had swollen, as did the numbers of civil servants, then and later. Indeed, one writer[1] indicates that during 1960 and 1961, 150,000 were added to the federal civil service, in 1962 a further 100,000 and in 1963 120,000, in a process of uncontrolled, unproductive growth. Quadros' investigations linked Goulart's name directly to the misappropriation of state pension funds, initiating an angry quarrel between the President and his Vice-President[2], which was only patched up later.

Quadros turned to the problems of financial recovery. Retrenchment at home and abroad was the order of the day. Simultaneously, he launched a drive against the contraband trade, particularly in coffee exports, which was costing the treasury a great deal of money. While endeavouring to impose austerity in government, he turned to the international and foreign creditors, especially the U.S.A., for help to shore up the finances, successfully negotiating with the Kennedy administration the rescheduling of the Brazilian debts to American banks and obtaining a line of substantial new credits, the whole constituting a 2,000 m. dollar package. Meanwhile, Quadros introduced a series of exchange reforms in a bid to halt the depreciation of the currency and to contain inflation, which in

[1] J. C. Garcia-Zamor, 'An ecological approach to administrative reform', *International Review of Administrative Sciences,* Vol. XXV, 1969, No. 4, p. 317.

[2] Hispanic American Report, Stanford University, Institute of Hispanic and Luso-Brazilian Studies, July 1961, p. 451.

1961 was driving up the cost of living and increasing labour unrest.

It all looked like a good beginning and public confidence began to grow. After this promising start on a range of urgent problems, Quadros began to move uncertainly towards more developmental policies. In foreign affairs he moved towards an independent nationalist policy, in an attempt to reduce reliance on the U.S.A.; he also began to foster trade relations with Eastern Europe and, finally, awarded the highest Brazilian decoration to 'Che' Guevara, then Cuban Minister for Industry. Quadros had no time for the politicians, made no real attempt to cultivate the support of the major groups and got on their nerves. Faced by the potentially hostile opposition of the PSD and the PTB in Congress, which took little or no action on the legislation Quadros sent in, he never actually brought matters to the clash that would probably have occurred sooner or later. Almost everything that he started aroused the hostility of vested interests —the tightening up of tax collection and the announcement of his intention to embark on land reform being two further examples. Unfortunately, he lacked staying power and after a few months in office was already at the end of his tether.

Quadros was to disappoint bitterly all those who had placed their hopes in him. A victim of his own unstable temperament, he abruptly resigned—possibly in the hope that popular pressure would bring him back again with greatly increased powers. Complaining of the terrible forces ranged against him, which had made it impossible for him to govern, he packed his bags seven months after taking office and left the country. The Congress in Brasília, having accepted the resignation, rapidly declared the Presidency vacant and installed the speaker of the Chamber of Deputies as interim President. Quadros' sudden abandonment of the Presidency was a severe moral blow to public opinion and it opened a crisis of the utmost gravity. The man who under the constitution was to assume the Presidency was the Vice-President, João Goulart, the leading figure of the Brazilian Labour Party, a former Minister of Labour and the recognized heir of the Vargas political tradition. At the time of Quadros' resignation he was on an official visit to Communist China.

Coming from the same frontier town in Rio Grande do Sul as Vargas, Goulart was of a well-to-do ranching family and was to become a considerable landowner in his own right, with an acute sense of the need to acquire more land and make more money; he was probably at his happiest on horse-back (even if his limp did come from a fall), wearing the long, baggy riding breeches of the gaúchos or appraising the weight and market price of prize cattle. In his youth he managed the family ranch and trained as a lawyer, but his friendly relations with Vargas brought him into politics, and Goulart campaigned for him in the 1950 election, becoming a federal deputy and later president of the Labour Party.

His appointment as Labour Minister of the Vargas regime in 1953 alarmed the middle classes and the military, who considered him a demagogue, and his recommendation to double the minimum wage, held to be inflationary, increased distrust of him among businessmen and industrialists. Vargas accordingly dropped him from the cabinet less than a year after his appointment, but Goulart was later back in the limelight as Vice-President, first in the Kubitschek regime and then under Jânio Quadros. Goulart, 'Jango' as everybody called him, entered Brazilian politics in the Vargas school, acquiring some of his master's skill in manoeuvre and the popular touch, being adept at talking on equal terms with farm hands or trade union leaders. Some regarded him as 'primário' ('thick') but he was accustomed to put on an act of ingenuousness in order to draw his interlocutor on; indecisive, he was astute enough in negotiation. While his friends commended him as modest ('humilde') and flexible, avoiding complete commitment to groups or ideologies, his enemies considered him as corrupt and a man without principles.

There was an immediate reaction to the possibility of Goulart becoming President. The three military ministers serving in the Quadros administration told the President of the Congress in Brasília that the return of Goulart to Brazil was absolutely undesirable for reasons of national security. In a joint note, they forecast that in the Presidency, with its ample personal powers, Goulart would represent the clearest form of encouragement to all those who wished to see the country engulfed by chaos, anarchy and civil strife; that the armed forces themselves, infiltrated and subdued, would, as had happened in other countries, be transformed into mere Communist militia. The ministers appeared to have been studying the case of Cuba, where the revolution had destroyed the regular army.

The ministers were unable, however, to make the warning

effective. There were strongly legalistic elements among the military, who were not united in a determination to keep Goulart out and there were also sectors of public opinion which, while not supporting him, nevertheless felt that the Constitution must be respected and that he must be given a chance. His brother-in-law, Leonel Brizola, governor of Rio Grande do Sul, took forceful steps to mobilize support for his office-taking, and received the backing of the army commander in the state capital, who defied the orders of the War Minister; the country was moving towards civil war. Public opinion, however, moved in Goulart's favour and he was able to take office but, as a compromise to meet the hostility towards him, a parliamentary system of government with a prime minister was established as a safeguard. This experiment, which Goulart himself worked to undermine, was a failure and, three prime ministers later, he recovered his full presidential powers by means of a national plebiscite early in 1963, with a large majority.

Goulart's skills proved to be no match for the problems piling up, which were both political and economic. He had recovered his Presidential powers but the deadlock that the Quadros regime had suffered in its relations with Congress continued, with the latter applying consistent delaying tactics, shelving for a year a land reform bill sent to it by the executive, amongst other measures. His tolerance of and co-operation with the Communists and left-wing radicals increased distrust of his intentions among the middle classes, which feared, rightly or wrongly, extremist measures by the Left. Throughout its last two years, the regime was weak, its authority corroded by its own lack of cohesion and by the attacks of its enemies, led, as always, by Carlos Lacerda.

Faced by growing economic and financial problems, Goulart hesitated to alienate his political supporters by taking the tough measures required. The test of his determination came in his attitudes to the stabilization policy of his Finance Minister, San Tiago Dantas, and to the Three Year Plan drawn up by a leading economist, Celso Furtado, in the name of the 'positive Left'. Furtado had already made a name for himself as head of the Superintendency for North-eastern development; an economist and writer on Brazilian problems, he was one of the Left's leading intellectuals, regarding himself however as a technician and remaining out of the main stream of politics. His Three Year Plan was ambitious in combining a high level of economic growth with a rapid reduction of the rate of inflation, and in stressing the need for determined short-term measures and for structural reforms.

Dantas, a Brazilian Labour party politician from Minas Gerais, was a man of action and it was he who took on the task of negotiating the acceptance of the reform programme and, largely, of explaining it to the public. Dantas launched energetically into the task of convincing the Americans, whose financial support was indispensable, of the value of the programme and the seriousness of the government's intentions, a task on which he worked with Roberto Campos, then Brazilian ambassador in Washington. Dantas obtained a measure of cautious support, subject to conditions, whereas, because of the critical situation at home, what he needed was whole-hearted backing both from the Americans and the International Monetary Fund. At home, his policies came under fierce attack both from the Right and the 'negative Left' and Dantas soon found that the necessary political support was being rapidly eroded. Goulart found how politically unpopular it was to enforce measures to reduce inflation and, fearing above all the competition from the extreme Left, did not wait long before abandoning policies of stabilization and taking the opportunity to secure the resignation of all his ministers and bring other men into the cabinet.

By the end of 1963 the principal indicators pointed to impending economic and financial catastrophe. Inflation, by transferring real resources from the consuming to the producing sector of the economy[1], had favoured the accumulation of capital for industrial expansion from the '50s onwards; it now became increasingly a sterile process of spiralling prices and costs, dangerous to the whole community.

Further aggravated by the crisis of Quadros' resignation, inflation, as measured by the annual rise in working classes' living costs in Rio, had shot up from 55 per cent in 1962 to 81 per cent in 1963. The federal budget was heavily in deficit and there was also a sizeable deficit in the balance of payments. Brazil's foreign debt had soared and her obligations to foreign creditors to be paid in 1964 were equivalent to a year's exports. In 1963 Brazil was plunging into chaos with the rate of economic growth, barely over 2 per cent, now lower than its 2.9 per cent

[1] David M. Trubek, *Law, Planning and Development of the Brazilian Capital Market,* New York University, April 1971, p. 17.

population growth. Industrial production, which had risen by 8 per cent in 1962, was hit by strikes, power cuts and import restrictions, growing by less than 3 per cent; output actually fell in the pace-making motor-vehicle industry and in textiles. The flow of foreign investment almost completely dried up.

Constant labour troubles, with some 90 strikes in 1963 alone, unrest in the rural areas, including invasion of the big estates by land-hungry impoverished peasants, increased the general feeling of insecurity. Without the heart to tackle the immediate economic problems, President Goulart turned to the question of basic reforms and, having failed to back his advisers of the 'positive Left', turned to the political forces of the extreme Left, led by the forceful Leonel Brizola, creator of the armed revolutionary action units, the 'groups of eleven'. During March 1964, his last month in office, Goulart, as if sensing that his days as President were numbered, took the radical political stance and decreed the measures that persuaded the waverers that he must go. Making an all-out bid to mobilize the masses and gain full support from the unions, Goulart called an open-air, mass meeting on March 13th in Cristiano Otoni Square in Rio, filled with over 100,000 workers from industrial and agricultural unions.

The General Command of Labour, which was not a legally constituted body, had placed all workers on the alert and called on them to attend the 'rally of the reforms'. They descended on Rio from the country and the cities, by special buses and trains with their fares paid, over 30,000 coming from São Paulo alone. Packing the huge square, which houses the main Rio railway station and the War Ministry, they carried banners with a variety of stirring slogans, such as: 'Jango! We'll defend your reforms with bullets', 'Jango! Sign the land reform bill and we'll take care of the rest' and 'Jango! Lock up the exploiters of the people'. They wanted uncompromising measures and the President did his best for them. Protected by massive contingents of police and soldiers, and invoking the memory of Getúlio Vargas, he announced the expropriation of the private oil refineries, and the signing of a decree taking over lands adjacent to federal roads and railways; he also called for profound modifications of the Constitution and the end of privileges for a small landowning minority. Brizola demanded the calling of a constituent assembly that would replace Congress and carry out wholesale reforms.

The middle classes of Rio, glued to their television or radio sets in the south zone of the city, took in all this with growing consternation. More of the same was to follow. Within 48 hours, Goulart sent a message to Congress requiring votes for illiterates, the eligibility of NCOs for elective posts and the legalization of the Communist party. While the military and civilian conspirators were gaining a mass of new, frightened adherents thanks to the impact of Goulart's offensive, the middle classes hit back in São Paulo on March 19th, the day of Saint Joseph, patron saint of the family, with a huge demonstration, the 'March of the family with God for freedom', in which over 500,000 people took part.

The military finally moved to depose President Goulart on March 31st 1964 for two basic reasons. The first was their alarm at the lack of effective government, shown in the events and circumstances discussed above. The second was the subversion of discipline in the armed forces.

President Goulart, like almost every other Brazilian President, believed in the need to cultivate support among the armed forces, to have his own 'dispositivo militar' of officers loyal to him and backing his policies. In his appointments to the top commands and in promotions, he endeavoured to favour those with known left-wing sympathies. Surprisingly, however, he went further than this in deciding to build himself a power base among the non-commissioned officers, to counter-balance the power of the officer corps and to create a pressure group that would ally itself with organized labour to back his reform programme. To this end he permitted, even encouraged, the infiltration of Communist and left-wing elements into the three services. The consequences of his policy were signs of ferment in the ranks and of the weakening of military discipline.

In September 1963, there was a revolt of several hundred navy, air force and marine NCOs and other ranks in Brasília against a Federal Supreme Court decision that they were not eligible for elective office. The rebels, who were in contact with the radical labour leaders, briefly took control of the city until they were subdued by the local garrison; President Goulart declined to take a stand against them. The reaction of the officer corps to events of this sort was vigorous and a well-organized network of conspiracy, which had existed in embryo for some time, now took firm root throughout the country.

Further confused events in October indicated that neither Goulart nor his military staff now had control of the armed forces. There were growing political pressures from both the Left and the Right and Carlos Lacerda, now governor of Guanabara (greater Rio), took the opportunity to give an inflammatory interview to an American press correspondent in which, as was his custom, he vilified the Goulart regime. On the urging of his three military ministers, the President applied to Congress for authority to declare a state of siege, and simultaneously the regime instructed the paratroops in Rio to arrest Lacerda.

The order misfired. The paratroop officers detailed to carry it out baulked and spent as long as they could discussing it amongst themselves and with their superiors; meanwhile one of them tipped off Lacerda as to what was in train. The arrest was never made, nor was a similar move to arrest Miguel Arraes, the left-wing governor of Pernambuco, who was to be detained because he symbolized mobilization on the Left as Lacerda did on the Right[1]. Goulart was reported to have said, months later, that he had been deposed, not on March 31st, but on the day in Rio when he had given orders to the paratroop unit and nobody had carried them out[2].

At a comparatively late stage, the military conspiracy came to be organized and articulated, in its military and to a good extent its civilian aspects, by the chief of staff of the armed forces, General Castello Branco, an officer of considerable prestige in the army, who not only had an office at the War Ministry but also one in Rio's Copacabana district, from which he directed the conspiracy. On March 20th, a week after the mass rally in Cristiano Otoni Square, he sent out from the Ministry a circular letter to all commands, denying army support to the plan of action proclaimed at the rally.

Castello was well known in the army for his legalism and for going 'by the book'; his views were therefore likely to influence moderate opinion among the officer corps. The letter referred to two threats: the calling of a constituent assembly to obtain the basic reforms and the intensifying of general agitation by the illegal power of the General Command of Labour. The armed forces were being called on to support these measures, Castello said, but it would be contrary to their duty to do so. They should be ready to defend the proper functioning of the three constitutional powers and of the laws, including those supporting the electoral process; they should be against a revolution

[1] T. E. S. Skidmore, *Politics in Brazil,* p. 263.
[2] *Os Idos de Março,* p. 283.

to establish a dictatorship and a constituent assembly, against the public calamity to be unleashed by the GCL and against the deformation of the historic role of the armed forces.

Events now moved to a climax. Goulart's Navy Minister, Admiral Mota, decided to punish the leaders of the Association of Sailors and Marines in Rio for taking part in political meetings in defiance of the regulations, and to dissolve their Association. The Admiral told the President of his intentions and that he was determined to carry them out in the interests of discipline; Goulart advised him not to do so. The sailors and marines who had recently enjoyed a special showing at the Education Ministry of the Russian revolutionary film *The Battleship Potemkin,* rebelled against the Admiral's decision, evading arrest, and led by Corporal Anselmo dos Santos, a 25-year-old political activist, they took refuge in the building of the Metalworkers' Union, where they were joined by trade union leaders sympathetic to their cause. A detachment of marines sent to arrest the mutineers failed to do so, some of them joining the mutiny; the officer commanding the Marines, Admiral Cândido Aragão, known for his political sympathies as the 'Red Admiral', had baulked at giving the marines their orders; the Navy Minister ordered his arrest. The army authorities were then told to arrest the mutineers. Goulart then fired the Navy Minister and appointed a new minister of left-wing sympathies, who promptly released the marine Admiral and pardoned the mutineers.

This frontal attack on military discipline proved to be the last straw. The military conspirators, who had stayed their hand until then, now found the armed forces as a whole ready to depose the President, Goulart's conduct in the crisis of the navy having alienated all but a few of the officers loyal to him. It was also the signal for which the conspirators had been waiting; officers and civilian liaison men were sent off to give the final instructions to groups throughout the country that were waiting for the signal.

The General Command of Labour made what was to be its last declaration on March 30th, warning that in four states the state governors were preparing a coup d'état with the aid of elements of the 2nd and 3rd armies. The Command claimed that the workers, prepared and united, would bar the way and announced the calling of a general strike. A few hours after Goulart had made his last public appearance as President at an NCOs meeting in the Rio Automobile Club, the military, with the middle classes solidly behind them and the workers passive, went into action throughout Brazil on March 31st 1964.

The Military revolt

Early on March 31st 1964 federal troops at Juiz de Fora and Belo Horizonte in the state of Minas Gerais, in close concert with the state governor, rebelled against the federal government.

They were led by two Mineiro generals, recently appointed by the President to commands in their home state—General Mourão Filho, who had been secretly conspiring against him since 1962, and General Guedes, who superstitiously hurried to advance the D-day of the revolt, originally set for April 2nd; March 31st was the end of the full moon and he never started anything serious when it was on the wane. The two generals had found a ready ally in Governor Magalhães Pinto, a canny, moderate Mineiro politician and banker who had watched with dismay and attempted to restrain the radicalization of politics nationally and in Minas, where clashes between the conservatives and the Left became increasingly sharp and numerous during the first quarter of 1964. The Governor had for some time been following a cagey political line, keeping open his communications with President Goulart but watching his moves with growing suspicion, and meanwhile maintaining contact with the conspirators, including General Castello Branco. Having long calculated on the possibility of having to organize resistance in Minas against the Goulart regime and finally convinced that composition with it was no longer possible, the governor persuaded the conspirators of Minas' strategic importance, either as a base for resistance or for an armed counter-offensive.

The events of March removed any doubts that the governor or the two generals held, and the revolt started in Minas. Manifestos were issued to the people, additional transport was commandeered and fuel supplies were placed under guard. While the police arrested left-wing union leaders and the governor secured their rearguard, the two generals moved their forces out on the roads to Brasília, the federal capital, and Rio de Janeiro, the political nerve centre. Before midnight, they were already on the border of the state of Rio.

For various reasons, events did not move as quickly in São Paulo, although the governor, Adhemar de Barros, had for some time been preaching revolt. General Kruel, the 2nd Army commander, had served under Goulart as War Minister, and spent the best part of a day urging the President to rid himself of pro-Communist associates, with Goulart replying that he could not cast aside the popular forces that supported him. Failing to obtain the assurances that he wanted, the general ordered his troops to march on Rio, join with the units advancing from Minas and prepare for an expected clash with pro-government forces. Police and army intelligence began to round up left-wing leaders. The Paulista trade unions declared their support for the General Command of Labour. Bank workers called a three day strike, the railway workers struck briefly and sabotaged railway equipment in defence of Goulart's mandate, the harbour and factories in Santos stopped working; but in São Paulo itself business and industry was near to normal working. Trade union offices remained closed and their leaders disappeared. Meanwhile, the military revolt was now spreading throughout the principal states of the Centre-South and the North-East.

In Rio where General Castello Branco was coordinating the operations of the rebellion, President Goulart, unaware of what was happening around him and over-confident of the support that he expected to receive from the First Army, reacted slowly to the march of events. His adversary, Carlos Lacerda, had shut himself in the Governor's palace, concentrating around it the means of defence at his disposal, chiefly the military police force, blocking the roads with the city's refuse-disposal trucks and expecting an attack that never came. In the city, the summons to the workers to stage a general strike fell flat, partly owing to the apathy of the workers and partly to the speed with which Lacerda's police locked up the union leaders. As the citizens of Rio took the rebellion largely in their stride, listening to its progress with their transistor radios on the beaches and in the streets, infantry and artillery from the 1st Army loyal to Goulart moved off towards Minas from the Rio garrison and the nearby city of Petrópolis.

Goulart's fate was decided when the troops sent from Rio to suppress the uprising met, parleyed and joined forces with the regiments from Minas and São Paulo. The civil war, predicted by some, never materialized and indeed Goulart seemed to realize rapidly that his cause was hopeless and to set his face against a military clash or any form of civil war. By April 2nd, such support as there was for him had crumbled completely and the President passed rapidly through Brasília, where he tried in vain to hold a cabinet meeting, before flying to Pôrto Alegre in the far south. Here Brizola attempted to organize a show of resistance, but he was unable to persuade his brother-in-law to stay and fight it out and shortly he too went into exile in Uruguay, followed by large numbers of government officials, politicians and businessmen who expected to get short shrift from the new regime.

The revolution was lightning and virtually bloodless. The speed of its execution surprised everyone, including even its leaders, who had at one time planned for some three months of hostilities and had considered the need to request foreign countries to recognize a state of belligerence. The rapid collapse of the Goulart regime was remarkable. Goulart had himself hastened the end by the recklessness and divisiveness of his conduct of government during March 1964. In the event, the expected support from his own military following and from the trade unions, unable to mobilize the workers in an effective general strike, dissolved into nothing and when he fell, he was abandoned by all save a few. Even allowing for the opportunism of politicians quick to identify a lost cause, and for the Brazilian custom of avoiding bloodshed, this was surprising in view of the aggressive confidence shown by the Left during the final months of the Goulart regime.

The end of the regime marked the end of an era. In 1964, a system of government based on a liberal constitution, political parties and free elections broke down; the experiment in democracy begun late in 1945 had lasted just under 20 years.

It is discouraging to conclude from the events of this period and from the circumstances of the country that many of the conditions for democracy to take root and grow were lacking. Examples of these deficiencies were the high rate of illiteracy, the inadequacy of communications and the great differences in the level of development of the main regions. Strong institutions and strong, cohesive political parties were unlikely to flourish under these circumstances, and in practice did not do so. Voters opted for personalities not for programmes and policies, and politicians with some exceptions looked after narrow local interests. Despite a good deal of apathy, there was political participation in the cities where politicians seeking election as President or state governor wooed the mass vote, using the techniques of 'populism'; where middle-men delivered votes to the politicians in return for favours or services promised to the voters, and the economic interests used their money to secure election of their own representatives. In the rural areas, however, democracy was a sham, with the balloting often open and the peasants voting for the landowners' candidate.

Lacking in genuine 'grass-roots' activity, weak, numerous political parties added up to a weak Congress and to governments ill-equipped to resolve the problems of national underdevelopment that faced them. These inadequacies were reflected in the political crises of the period, as governments struggled vainly against corrosive forces, of which headlong inflation was the most powerful. The struggle was unequal and towards the end of the 20-year period it became increasingly difficult for governments or this narrowly-based, shaky democracy to survive.

3 Castello Branco: The Military in Government

The First Institutional Act

The troops engaged in the operations of the military rebellion returned to their barracks; the dust began to settle and Brazilians waited to see what would happen next.

A week elapsed before the leaders of the revolt set their intentions before the public. On April 9th the three military ministers of the provisional government set up on the departure of President Goulart issued an Institutional Act in the name of a revolutionary supreme command. From that day the Brazilian armed forces, led by the army as the senior service, took formal control of the country. The military, in exercising a moderating power, had frequently intervened in politics during the Republic but it had been their custom, after these interventions, to withdraw into the background. This time however they had come to stay and politics would never be the same again.

The first public document of the Movement of March 1964, the First Institutional Act, was a mixture of military bluntness and legalistic language. Constitutional processes had failed to depose the government, which was deliberately getting ready to bolshevize the country, the preamble said; the 'revolution' did not seek to secure its legitimacy through the action of Congress.

Besides these and other statements of the military viewpoint were texts written by the civilian lawyers, who presented the idea of a constituent power inherent in the 'revolution'. The only source of this power was the people, and the revolution's leaders, thanks to the action taken by the armed forces and the unmistakable support given by the nation, represented the people and exercised power in its name. The 'revolution' distinguished itself from other armed movements by interpreting the interests and wishes not of one group but of the nation.

The preamble of the Act spoke of the Movement's intentions and of the tasks ahead. The future government must have the means to embark on the economic, financial, political and moral reconstruction of Brazil, as well as to take immediate measures for resolving the serious and urgent problems on which the restoration of the country's internal order and international prestige depended. It was not intended to radicalize the revolutionary process and the 1946 constitution was therefore being maintained; but the powers of the future President were being modified to equip him to restore economic and financial order and to take urgent steps to drain the Communist abscess, the poison of which had reached the top levels of government and infiltrated the administration. The full powers assumed by the 'revolution', the preamble said, would be reduced by the maintenance of the Congress, with certain provisos concerning its powers.

In its 11 articles, the Act got down to specific measures. It ordered Congress to elect a new President and Vice-President by absolute majority within two days for terms of office ending in January 1966. It speeded up the law-making process, obliging Congress to consider constitutional amendments or draft laws proposed by the President within one month, failing which they would automatically become law; it gave the President the exclusive right to propose laws creating or raising public expenditure and forbade congressmen to submit amendments that would further increase it. The Act also suspended for six months constitutional or legal guarantees of life tenure and stability in posts, with the intention of purging and reducing the inflated ranks of the civil service. Finally, it gave the future regime ample powers to purge the political classes by annulling elective mandates and suspending political rights for ten years, granting these powers for two months only. The Act was to be valid until January 31st 1966.

It had two prominent features: anti-Communism and distrust of the politicians.

The military leaders apparently considered that Brazil, with its weak economy, political immaturity and low level of culture, was especially vulnerable to Communist infiltration. For the outside observer, it was however difficult to assess the validity of their fears or to measure the actual strength of Communism in Brazil, which existed as a clandestine organization; moreover, after 1964 'Communist' seemed to become a more elastic term.

The Brazilian Communist party had been operating underground since its prohibition in 1947 after only two years of legality. It continued in the 1950s to organize cadres and hold party congresses and, since it controlled a proportion of working-class votes, was usually courted at election times by politicians, including presidential candidates, counting their likely adherents.

Under its veteran leader Luís Carlos Prestes, faithful to the Soviet line, the party worked to recover legal status and to this end was prepared to make the necessary electoral deals. Not all the Communists liked Prestes' leadership and in the early '60s various groups, holding allegiance to the Chinese or Cuban lines, broke off from the main party.

The Communists began to enjoy much easier circumstances when Goulart became President in 1961. 'Jango', though certainly not a Communist, had frequently worked with their leaders and claimed that he knew how to handle them. For Prestes at least, this seemed to present the opportunity to win back legal status, and he therefore supported the various moves towards establishing a broad popular front of left-wing forces to back the Goulart government. The early '60s were years of increasing Communist activity, including participation in the innumerable strikes, with the Communists building up their cadres in the new rural unions and stepping up the pace of infiltration in the civil service, the universities and the armed forces. Prestes expressed satisfaction at the extent of the progress achieved during this period.

The degree of unrest among the NCOs of the armed forces during 1963, with indiscipline reaching its peak in the naval mutiny of March 1964, indicated some success in the left wing campaign among the armed forces, in which no doubt the Communists shared. The military, in the First Institutional Act provided for the purging of their own ranks; later, they set up an investigating group under a colonel, assisted by 20 officers and NCOs, to document and analyse the Communists movement's activities.

The Act reflected military disillusionment with the politicians. Looking at the state of the nation, many of the military had decided that Brazilian society had failed to produce authentic political parties with valid programmes to meet the national problems. They had looked at the politicians individually and usually disliked what they saw. Talk to an army officer about them and, rubbing his thumb on his index finger, he would express the opinion that Brazilian party politics were based on bribery and corruption. This attitude was to be a thread running through military thinking from 1964 onwards, and in future crises, major or minor, the purging of politicians at the national or state level frequently accompanied the various measures taken by the Executive.

The new President

Duly elected by Congress on April 11th 1964, the new President was General Humberto de Alencar Castello Branco, the leader of the military conspiracy, little known in civilian circles but enjoying considerable prestige in the army.

Born in 1900 at Fortaleza, capital of the state of Ceará, Castello's roots were in the other Brazil of the North-East, his Portuguese ancestors having first settled in nearby Piauí. Castello received his early schooling in Fortaleza, but later moved south when the duties of his father, who was a brigadier, took the family to Rio. Physically, he was very much the Cearense. The squat head—the 'cabeça chata' that is a characteristic of people from that State—rose out of broad shoulders, while spinal trouble made a short neck look even shorter. His associates considered him genuinely Cearense in other respects, his quickness of mind confirming the truth of the saying that there was no such thing as a naïve Cearense. Austere and frugal—he ate sparingly and drank only to keep others company—he seemed to embody the spartan qualities that the North-easterner acquires in a harsh environment that places a premium on the capacity to survive. He had a Cearense's obstinacy and when he wanted something, did not stop until he got it.

Until he became President and went on the reserve list, Castello spent all his life in the army, in which he served for 43 years. From his youth, when he went to one of the best military schools, in Pôrto Alegre, he rose steadily and attended the courses abroad reserved for outstanding officers—the Ecole Supérieure de Guerre in France and the General Staff course in the U.S.A. As a Lieutenant-Colonel he went to Italy in the Second World War with the Brazilian Expeditionary Force, of which he was the chief of operations, serving in the American Fifth Army with a number of Brazilian officers who were later to be prominent in Brazilian life and whose attitudes to their country's problems were moulded by their experience overseas.

Castello's interests outside army life were wide. Addicted to reading and classical music, he went often to the theatre, and when President would go back-stage to chat with the artists. On one occasion a group of hot-headed officers expressed their intention of acting forcefully against a Rio theatre showing a play that they considered offensive to the armed forces. Castello lost no time and went to a performance, later instructing General

Costa e Silva, the War Minister, to tell the officers that they were wrong and had no business setting themselves up as censors.

Socially, he was a man of few words with people he did not know. Courteous but maintaining a degree of reserve unusual among Brazilians, he was alien to the backslapping approach of the 'abraço', but he was gallant with the opposite sex and liked to dress well. He was open with people he knew and, the better he knew them, the more ironical; but one of his associates found him sarcastic and on occasions he could be 'crusty'. He drew his close friends from among those who had shared the same career, men like Cordeiro de Farias, Adhemar de Queiroz and Lyra Tavares. A family man, he was devoted to the memory of his wife, Dona Argentina, who died in Recife in 1963; early on the day that he was to assume the Presidency in Brasília, he visited her grave at the cemetery in Rio, before boarding the presidential Viscount at Santos Dumont airport.

Journalists did not like his press conferences, carefully managed occasions in which he read out answers to written questions, setting a pattern that later Presidents were to follow. At times it seemed that the press 'en masse' got on his nerves. One such occasion was a luncheon given in his honour by the foreign correspondents' club in Rio. Michael Field, the president of the club, asked each correspondent to introduce himself, giving his name and his newspaper or agency. Castello was on edge. The turn came round to one of the Soviet correspondents who facetiously introduced himself as one of the 'subversives'. Castello snapped back that he was grateful for the information and would certainly tell the police to keep an eye on him; later at question-time he rapped out a curt answer to an American correspondent. Further experience of him showed however that he was well able to unbend to journalists individually and display an ironic sense of humour, after an initial reserve that he would drop after he had sized his visitors up.

He was intent on restoring the prestige and dignity of the Presidency, which had sunk low under Jânio Quadros and João Goulart. It was typical of him that on assuming office he made a voluntary declaration of his assets, modest as they were. When he left it, Brazilians, who normally assume that the President lines his own pocket and that of his friends, seemed to be convinced that Castello had not done so. Without a popular vote behind him, he nevertheless had a keen sense of responsibility to the great mass of under-privileged Brazilians.

Castello brought to the conduct of government qualities derived from his military upbringing. He knew how to give orders and had authority, as well as the staff officer's habits of teamwork. An energetic man propelled by a military sense of duty, he was able to work long hours that would have tired out men less resilient; he lived and worked by the clock, a very rare thing among Brazilians. He needed these qualities when he assumed the Presidency in April 1964, inheriting a situation marked by administrative chaos and a pressing need for leadership.

Castello's cabinet was one of top civil servants, diplomats and veteran revolutionary figures well known as the 'Lieutenants' of the 1930s, such as Juarez Távora and Cordeiro de Farias, men who were also closely associated with the War College (Escola Superior de Guerra) of which Castello had been an instructor and director of studies.[1] General Costa e Silva remained as War Minister from the provisional government, the Foreign Ministry went to an experienced professional diplomat, Vasco Leitão da Cunha, and the posts of Finance and Planning Ministers went to Octávio Gouveia de Bulhões, a civil servant and university professor, and to Roberto de Oliveira Campos, an economist and former ambassador in Washington. With the exception of the Vice-President, José Maria Alkmim, who came from the Social Democratic Party (PSD) the civilian political figures in the cabinet were of the National Democratic Union (UDN). As a governmental team, it was cohesive, hard-working and prepared to take unpopular decisions; international in its outlook, it regarded Brazil as an integral part of the Western alliance and co-operated with the U.S.A.

The early months of the new regime were dominated by the wholesale purge carried out on a broad front and involving the arrest and detention without trial of many actual or imagined opponents. Its intensity and scope, which surprised public opinion, reflected the determination of the military to weed out those men, military or civilian, who in their opinion had contributed to the imminent collapse of the country in 1964. Thus on April 11th, the day when Castello was elected to the Presidency, over 120 officers were formally expelled from the armed forces and the purges continued throughout the year.[2] The expulsions

[1] The activities of the War College are discussed in Chapter 5.

[2] Alfred Stepan, *The Military in Politics,* p. 223.

were most numerous in the army, where they were directed by General Costa e Silva; they were accompanied by measures to promote officers whose advancement had been held back for their stand against Goulart, and to stop promotion of those not in step with the Movement of March 1964. It was the first time that the military had purged their ranks for political reasons.

The political classes simultaneously felt the axe. Article 10 of the Institutional Act provided, without the right of appeal, for the suspension of political rights and the cancelling of parliamentary mandates for ten years. Congressmen, state governors and former Presidents were among those proscribed, including ex-Presidents Goulart, Quadros and Juscelino Kubitschek, always a popular figure in Brazil, but a representative of the old political order and the party machines that were anathema to many of the military. Among leading intellectuals who lost their political rights were Celso Furtado and Josué de Castro, a sociologist and expert on problems of nutrition.

The powers given by Article 10 were to be used for only the first two months of the new regime. On their expiry, the regime's punitive action for the next three months centred on Article 7, which gave it authority to dismiss, suspend and pension holders of public office, after the carrying out of summary investigations. This was the main instrument in removing alleged subversive and corrupt elements from the civil service and the armed forces, and by the time of its expiry on October 9th a total of some 4,450 persons at all levels had been punished under its provisions. In the various ministries and other federal or state agencies, its incidence varied with the degree of determination of the ministers, state governors or administrative chiefs.

A period of experiment

The armed forces took power without having prepared a plan or programme of political action. The First Institutional Act, with its punitive clauses and its statement of general intentions, was hardly a blueprint for government; it was left to Castello to attempt to give a political direction to the Movement of March 1964. He did so in the light of his own convictions and under the particular circumstances of the time; political power was now being directly exercised by the military, with all the stresses and strains that this would involve in the future.

It was said of Castello that he was the most 'civilian' of the

Brazilian generals. Legalistic in his outlook, he was best suited to be a constitutional President; far from being hungry for power, he seemed to regard his role as that of a temporary custodian, who must put a dilapidated estate in order and hand it over, restored and solvent, to its rightful owner. He initially resisted but later accepted a move to extend his term of office by just over a year to March 1967. In this reluctance, Castello wished to set an example that would help check the abuses of holding on to power; more than once during his Presidency, he spoke out against 'continuism', the habit manifested in Vargas of perpetuating ones self in office. Highly critical of what he regarded as the demagogy of Brazilian politicians, he obstinately held out against any form of self-advertisement, to the extent that he was criticized for failure to communicate his policies to the public.

Believing in the superiority of democracy as a form of government, Castello was obliged by circumstances to be an authoritarian. He nevertheless tried to keep all the options open for a return to democratic government, considering that an attempt should be made to reform the political institutions and modernize them. He was therefore ready to work with Congress, to receive and talk with politicians and to exercise a parliamentary type of political leadership, as far as this was possible. Thus, one of his earliest acts was to arrange the formation of a government bloc in the Chamber of Deputies. This was built around the National Democratic Union (UDN), the only one of the three major parties that could be said genuinely to support the Movement of March 1964, and was reinforced by elements from the Social Democratic Party (PSD), the party created by Getúlio Vargas. Possessed of political skill, Castello went to work on the tasks of government with apparent confidence that he could carry the armed forces with him and win the civilian politicians over to his viewpoint. His strategy was based on three objectives: to maintain the working of Congress, preserve the integrity of the Federal Supreme Court and guarantee the freedom of the press. However, he was able to secure only the last of these objectives fully throughout his term of office.

If 1964 was the year of the purges, 1965 seemed to promise more constructive measures. Political events moved at a steady pace during the first half of the year, reflecting a presidential statement that 1965 was to be a year of political reform and the correction of political distortions. Governmental efforts were directed towards maintaining an atmosphere of stability in which a political reform programme could be prepared and implemented. Castello took various opportunities to declare the regime's determination to continue on a middle course.

The regime's confidence was shown by its decision to hold elections for governor in 11 states at the end of 1965, and by its approval of the holding of municipal elections in São Paulo at the end of March. In these, Brigadier Faria Lima with the support of ex-President Jânio Quadros—still active despite the loss of his political rights—was elected to the post of Mayor by a large majority.

This was a period of calm, in which there was no real threat to the Castello Branco administration's control over events. One incident, however, involving Miguel Arraes, the ex-governor of Pernambuco, revealed a fundamental problem facing the regime: the containing of the intransigence of some of the military within the limits of the law.

Arraes, an authentic figure of the Brazilian Left, had been detained by the army authorities since the coup d'état, being frequently questioned by the officers in charge of the military inquiry groups, but was at last granted a writ of habeas corpus by the Federal Supreme Court. Castello had to intervene to enforce Arraes' release and to cut short the expressions of mutual animosity by members of the Court and officers who were convinced that it was only too happy to pass down decisions unfavourable to the Movement of March 1964. In the event, Arraes received asylum in the Algerian embassy and later left the country.

During July 1965 the regime went ahead with the various preparations intended to further the process of 'redemocratization', an objective that Castello considered a predominant part of the Movement's programme. A Statute of the Political Parties was put through Congress, designed to reduce their number and compel them to reorganize on less 'club-like' lines. An Electoral Code was approved to tighten the electoral process, with particular reference to the elections for governor to be held in eleven states early in October.

There was nothing startling in these two measures, there being general agreement that a start had to be made in clearing away obstacles to the development of more mature forms of political organization. At the same time however a 'Law of Ineligibility' was put on the statute books, with the purpose of keeping out of the October elections candidates who would act as focal points for the gathering of counter-revolutionary forces. Some of the regime's critics advised consistently against holding elections on the grounds that they were premature, but the regime's political team, led by Castello, went ahead, disregarding the adverse climate caused by the government's austerity measures, especially by its programme to reduce inflation. The policy of an early return to more democratic government was to be given every opportunity of proving itself.

During August and September, the political parties made their arrangements for presenting candidates at the elections. The opposition, in general the Social Democrat (PSD) and Brazilian Labour Parties (PTB), had some difficulty in getting suitable candidates through the net of the Law of Ineligibility and, as a result of decisions by the electoral courts, one candidate was disqualified in Minas Gerais and two in Guanabara (the city-state of Rio de Janeiro). In the other states the difficulties were less. There was confusion as to what the elections were actually about. In a demonstration of political ingenuousness the federal government at one time declared that the 'revolution' was not really at stake in the elections and that they should be fought on local and not national issues. While this was a possibility in the more parochial atmosphere of the North-East, it proved to be a miscalculation in the context of developed areas such as Minas Gerais and Guanabara.

In the event, the polling day on October 3rd passed by without disturbance of the public order. The next day, however, sensing the victory of a candidate in Minas associated with him, and probably anxious to revenge himself on the Movement, which had deprived him of his political rights, ex-President Kubitschek returned in triumph to Rio from his exile in Paris; he was in time to witness the victory of the PSD/PTB coalition in the key states of Minas and Guanabara over the candidates of the National Democratic Union, the party closely associated with the regime. This was generally interpreted not as a victory for democracy but as a defeat for the Movement.

The election of two veteran politicians, Israel Pinheiro in Minas and Negrão de Lima in Guanabara was the catalyst for the building up of intense pressure on the Castello Branco government. These men represented the old political classes: Israel Pinheiro had been closely associated with Kubitschek, having been placed in charge of building operations at Brasília; Negrão de Lima had been an aide of Getúlio Vargas in the establishment of the semi-Fascist 'Estado Nôvo'. Nationalist officers of the 'hard line' and especially the younger ones wishing to sweep away the old order of things and to modernize and develop the country, if need be by authoritarian government and radical measures, considered that it was completely alien to the Movement's objectives for these two men to take office. Military pressures were therefore exerted upon Castello to annul the results of the elections and even, reportedly, to carry out investigations into the careers of the two men.

The crisis was marked by significant weakening of the armed forces' backing for Castello. Regimental commanders of the Rio garrison placed their units on alert and officers discussed what action should be taken; it was reported that a mechanized reconnaissance regiment was prepared to move against the regime.[1] At the height of the crisis, General Costa e Silva, who remained loyal to Castello, went down to the Vila Militar in Rio to persuade the officers not to withdraw their support from the government. It was a crucial time for military unity. Some officers felt that Castello was not being sufficiently radical nor taking a severe enough line with those who had no sympathy for the goals of the Movement of March 1964. In Congress, the politicians of the PSD prepared to come out into the open in their opposition to the regime and a portion of the UDN, led by Carlos Lacerda, began to get ready to deny its support.

Castello and Costa e Silva were forced to give an assurance that stern measures would be taken to safeguard the regime and impose its control. These were an expansion of federal powers over the states, strict measures to circumscribe the liberty of action of those deprived of their political rights (including ex-President Kubitschek) and a constitutional amendment to provide for the indirect election of the President by Congress.

At the end of October the stern measures were presented to Congress in the form of two messages, but there were no longer sufficient votes to ensure approval of the second message, which was in the form of a constitutional amendment and therefore required an absolute majority. The hitherto solid front of the UDN in support of the regime was now broken by a partial defection and the PSD, which had in the past shown pliability in giving the government approval of the legislation it needed, now decided that the regime was bluffing and that the bluff should

[1] Ibid, p. 255.

be called. In addition, there was a general realization that the messages represented only the beginning of the steps that the regime was bound to take and that there would be more to come.

The crisis was resolved by increased authoritarianism. The two opposition governors took office but the military critics were pacified by the issuing of a Second Institutional Act. This came at the end of October but had been germinating for nearly a month; both General Costa e Silva and Cordeiro de Farias had had texts drafted by two jurists, Gama e Silva and Vicente Rau, both of São Paulo. Castello hesitated for some time before signing but finally called the head of his civilian household, Luís Vianna Filho, at 5 a.m. one morning to say that he was ready to do so.

The Second Institutional Act

The Second Act, which followed the First by little more than 18 months, reintroduced the powers to purge the political classes and the civil service. It went even further however. The Judiciary, whose integrity Castello had hoped to preserve, was now to fall into line: the number of judges of the Federal Supreme Court was increased from 11 to 16, thus facilitating the formation of a majority that would not defy the Movement. The Executive won new powers to intervene in the states in order to prevent or suppress subversion of order or to ensure the execution of the federal laws. The new Act swept the traditional political parties off the board, and decreed that new ones be set up under the terms of the legislation passed in July 1965. In a further tightening of political control, it empowered the President to decree the recess of Congress, the state legislative assemblies or the municipal councils.

The Act also prepared for the handing over of power. Castello wrote a clause making himself ineligible for re-election and the Act laid down that the next presidential election would take place by absolute majority of the members of Congress on a date not later than October 3rd 1966. By setting the date of the Act's expiry as March 15th 1967, when the next government would take office, the regime indicated at least an intention of moving forward to something less authoritarian than yet another Institutional Act.

The new Institutional Act helped to repair the divisions within the Movement. The strength of military pressures had obliged Castello to give way and to revise his policies, a price that he was compelled to pay in the interest of the unity of the armed forces.

The aftermath

The sweeping powers now available to Castello made it possible to begin a more dynamic phase in government. Juracy Magalhães, a new Minister of Justice, acted as political coordinator and a series of measures were taken to strengthen the regime. These included the formation in Congress of the new political groupings of support for, or opposition to, the regime, entities that were subsequently constituted as the Aliança Renovadora Nacional (Arena), of which the nucleus was the former UDN, and the Movimento Democrático Brasileiro (MDB) built around the old PTB.

Castello's action in making himself ineligible for a second term of office left the question of the presidential succession wide open. In fact, however, General Costa e Silva's important role in helping to resolve the political crisis leading to the Second Institutional Act had made him the natural candidate. Early in January 1966, on the eve of a trip to Europe and through a politician close to him, he announced that he was prepared to run for the Presidency.

There is little doubt that Castello was aware that this step was going to be taken, but it seemed that his admiration for a colleague of more than forty years in the army stopped short of considering him as suitable to be the next President of Brazil. General Costa e Silva represented the conventional element of the officer class; his candidacy, therefore, implied a shift of power away from those who, like Castello, were closely associated with the War College and had a broader intellectual background.

In the event, what surprised many was the steam-roller power of the candidacy once it got under way after the War Minister's return from a visit to Europe. Strong support, with corresponding pressure on the executive of the Arena, came from the top military echelons, and others were simply brushed aside.

General Costa e Silva was therefore adopted as presidential candidate of the Arena by an overwhelming majority on May 26th and Pedro Aleixo, a Mineiro and a prominent member of the old UDN was elected his running mate; they were formally elected early in October.

Indirect elections for governor took place in 12 states in September 1966. Learning its lesson from the elections of October 1965, which brought defeat for the Movement in two key states, the regime made sure that there would be no trouble this time and directed that the elections be held in the states' legislative assemblies, where by means of the Arena their course could be properly controlled. Since the MDB under these conditions refused to take part, the governmental candidates were elected without opposition.

The scene was now set for the final round of elections in November, when the whole of the Chamber of Deputies, one third of the federal Senate and the entire state assemblies were to be renewed. This took place without incident on November 15th and was hailed by the regime as a victory; Castello promptly gave instructions to transform the Arena into a fully-fledged political party.

A new Constitution

It was typical of Castello that, having felt the impact of opinion in the armed forces, he tried to provide a framework within which a constitutional form of government could be conducted; he may well have seen the dangers of a move to outright dictatorship. In December 1966 he sent to Congress a new draft constitution, which was duly approved by Congress and entered into force in March 1967.

The new charter was intended to furnish General Costa e Silva with the necessary powers to govern effectively when he took over the Presidency. It maintained the provision of the Institutional Acts by which the President sent legislation to Congress for processing within one month, but restored to Congress the right to annul mandates and suspend the political rights of its own members; it established the indirect system of presidential election by an electoral college composed of Congress and representatives of the state legislative assemblies.

The new text broadened the institution of the state of siege in order to enable the President to deal with emergency situations and gave him stronger powers to discipline states that contravened the federal economic and financial policies or fell into financial disorder. Its purpose was to provide a good degree of political and administrative centralization. Pushed through Congress with a speed that left little time for adequate discussion, it liquidated the old federal system; the text abolished the old name of 'the United States of Brazil', the country being now called simply 'Brazil'. Congress itself was deprived of any real powers to obstruct or modify the policies of the administration, the responsibility for initiating, and following through, action on the country's problems being now entrusted to a strong Executive.

The preparations for assumption of power by the Costa e Silva administration were completed by two major pieces of legislation, the national security and press laws. These were both passed in the closing weeks of the outgoing administration, the national security law being published only a day before the handing over of power. The press law enacted in February was criticized by the Brazilian press, radio and television, which undertook a national campaign in protest and even mobilized support for their case from international associations of journalists. The security law, which was generally considered to represent the views on national problems of the War College was, similarly, ill received. It included among other things, powers to inflict stiff penalties on those trying to subvert the 'politico-social' order, to promote strikes in the public services or to publish false or tendentious news that would endanger the prestige or credit of Brazil. The combination of these two laws with the new constitution appeared to vest a formidable concentration of powers in the future President.

4 Castello Branco: Retrenchment and Reform

By the beginning of 1964, the consequences of long-standing disrespect for the principles of sound economic and financial management were being severely felt in Brazil. Inflation was accelerating and the destruction of the currency and of the country's credit abroad was imminent; if action had been delayed much longer, there would have been little to save from the wreckage.

The Castello Branco administration brought determination and staying-power to the tackling of the crisis. Although no expert in economics, Castello took full responsibility for economic and financial policy as he did for the other policies of his government; indeed, he would often say that they were his and that his ministers were carrying them out. In practice, he worked hard to grasp fully the intentions and implications of proposed measures, engaging in lengthy discussions with Roberto Campos, the Minister of Planning, and Professor Bulhões, the Finance Minister. There was mutual confidence between Castello and these two men, while the partnership between the two ministers, whose responsibilities could overlap and give rise to friction, was genuine and unaffected by Campos' emergence as the regime's principal spokesman in this sector.

Roberto de Oliveira Campos was born in Cuiabá, capital of the state of Mato Grosso and in the heart of the backlands of the Centre-West, but he was international in outlook and anything but a provincial. In his early years he studied for the Church, attending a seminary where training by the Jesuits contributed notably to his intellectual formation. He decided, however, that the Church was not his vocation and when he was 22 entered the foreign service. The 'Itamarati', as it is known in Brazil, taking its name from the old colonial palace in Rio that was until recently its headquarters, impresses as perhaps the best organized of Brazilian government services. In his early career, Campos was a member of Brazilian delegations at international conferences, working as economic counsellor at the United Nations. At home, his most important post, until he became Castello's Planning Minister, was with the National Bank for Economic Development, of which he became President in 1958, being later forced out by political pressure. It was during his work there that he joined Lucas Lopes, the Finance Minister, in drawing up the stabilization programme that President Kubitschek was to discard as incompatible with his development plans. The peak of Campos' diplomatic career was his appointment as Ambassador to Washington during the Quadros administration.

He was at his best in government, having the ability to form and work with a team, to delegate authority and deal in the same day with a host of different questions. Liberal and internationalist, he was a constant opponent of the attitudes of the political classes, and his addiction to logic and rigorous analysis made him a natural leader of the technocracy that from 1964 onwards was to have a fully-fledged opportunity to reshape the economic fortunes of Brazil. He believed in the benefits to be derived from foreign capital. Much of his career in the public service was spent in the United States, where he also trained as an economist. His American connections and admiration for U.S. standards of organization made him suspect to Brazilian nationalists, who tarred him with the 'pro-American' brush. His critics in Brazil could however hardly deny the intellectual gifts displayed in his writing, the talent for absorbing and relating to Brazil the experience gained in a broad range of foreign countries and for drawing lessons to assist in the solution of Brazilian problems.

Campos' partner in economic and financial management, Octávio Bulhões, was an economist and university professor, as well as a career civil servant in the Finance Ministry, with experience in representing Brazil at the U.N. and at the International Monetary Fund (I.M.F.) as Vice-Governor. Professor Bulhões was to play his part in preparing the financial reforms of the Castello Branco regime; respected for his integrity, he bore the burdens of a Ministry traditionally subject to innumerable pressures, where the casualty rate amongst the incumbents had been alarmingly high. By contrast, a feature of government from 1964 onwards was the degree of stability in the tenancy of the Finance Ministry, and the extent of the support given by successive Presidents to Professor Bulhões and his successor, Professor Delfim Neto (at the time of writing still in office). These were positive factors in the long-drawn campaign to curb inflation that lay ahead and was still not concluded in 1972.

The Brazilian disease

Chronic, deep-seated inflation began to take root in the post-depression years of the 1930s. Thereafter it was a permanent feature, except for a brief interlude at the end of the '40s when the cost of living was almost stabilized. The inflationary gallop began during the free-spending Kubitschek administration, when the printing presses worked overtime, and it reached breakneck speed in the Goulart regime. By the first quarter of 1964, it was proceeding at an annual rate of 140 per cent.

For most people, it is difficult to conceive how normal living could go on with such intense inflation; how wage-earners, despite the periodic readjustments, could cope with the sharp fluctuations in the real value of their earnings, or how housewives could run a home with the constant rise in prices. Neither manual nor white-collar workers fared well under inflation which, with the general difficulty of raising a family and paying the doctor's bills, fostered among Brazilians the habit of holding three jobs simultaneously.

With the currency rapidly depreciating, Brazilians stopped saving and put their money into real estate, durable consumer goods, short-term commercial paper yielding a quick return, or into building up their own private stocks of dollars—anything to protect their income against erosion. Pensioners and those living on fixed incomes suffered most since their adjustments invariably came late. The rich bought hard currencies and put them in bank accounts in Switzerland or the U.S.A. in amounts that were, for obvious reasons, never disclosed.

Inflation built into the economy a number of distortions that after 1964 were to prove hard to eradicate or modify. It drove private savings out of the stock-market, making it very difficult for firms to raise capital, and created a gap that the government could only partially fill through the official banks. It decapitalized private companies and distorted their accounting and in business life often made tax evasion and cheating the authorities the condition for survival. Nobody paid debts on time because subsequent rises in prices and increases in the money supply made it possible to repay in inflated, depreciated currency. The decline in value of money imposed severe strains on the balance of payments and led to frequent devaluations.

The basic cause of this Brazilian disease was government overspending and its consequence: inflationary issues of paper money to meet the deficit in the government accounts. Natural disasters such as droughts and floods, as well as the failure of food production, transport and distribution to meet the needs of the growing cities, contributed to the trend of rising prices.

The struggle for stabilization

In the Castello Branco regime's programme to tackle inflation, a fundamental choice had to be made at the outset. Was this chronic disease to be cured by a shock treatment, which was reputedly the method favoured by the experts of the I.M.F.; or was there to be a gradual treatment of its causes? Official spokesmen in due course announced that the government had opted for gradualism.

The decision was well received in Brazil, where many believed that, if the shock treatment cured inflation, it would certainly kill the patient in the process. Campos himself declared in the administration's Economic Action Programme for 1964-66 (PAEG) that the success of a shock treatment depended on a general freezing of wages and salaries, which would be socially undesirable, because some classes had recently received increases whereas others had not. He said that such treatment involved abrupt changes in the demand for goods and services, which would lead to price rises and unemployment; that it was better to allow business and industry, whose operations had been vitiated by years of inflation, to return to health after a period of convalescence, rather than bring them to bankruptcy; and that the success of a shock treatment required the rapid elimination of public sector deficits, which could not be achieved without considerable reduction of public investments.

The decision on how to tackle inflation was accompanied by one on the resumption of growth. Campos' aims, set forth in the PAEG, were ambitious: to surmount the economic stagnation of 1963, to resume in 1965 and 1966 the average annual growth rate of 6 per cent obtained from 1947 to 1961, and to create conditions to raise it to 7 per cent. Brazil had consciously set out to pursue two objectives simultaneously: the resumption of development and the reduction of inflation. It was to prove a difficult exercise in reconciliation.

Within this overall policy, the two ministers took various related measures. Action was concentrated on the reduction of the budget deficit and the control of wage increases. The administration from April 1964 onwards faced the hurdle of cutting the huge deficit inherited from the Goulart regime, of progressively narrowing the gap between expenditure and revenue until this source of inflationary pressure could be eliminated. The means to achieve this were the pruning of expenses, a shut-down on new public works and the reduction of subsidies to uneconomic government transport companies. Non-inflationary funds were to be raised to finance the deficit and revenue was to be increased by more effective taxation.

For Brazilians, not the least painful aspect of the new austerity was to be the tightening of the grip in taxation. Tax payment in Brazil had never had the seriousness peculiar to it in Anglo-Saxon countries. Accommodation with the tax collector was seldom a problem for the rich and there was always skilled legal advice available to indicate any loopholes in the law and increase the margin of safety for tax evaders. Tax receipts in São Paulo and Rio were too low to be true. In October 1964, Castello dismissed 108 tax inspectors in São Paulo in a lightning clean-up following investigations in the regional tax office.

The regime later put bills through Congress to define tax evasion and fix penalties for those caught filing false returns, and served notice that it would take into consideration outward signs of wealth such as country houses, cars, boats and aircraft for the taxpayer's personal use, racing stables, lavish standards of entertaining and foreign travel. Correcting a surprising piece of generosity by past governments, it cancelled the income tax exemption enjoyed by journalists, teachers and magistrates. It also set tax deduction at source on a firm basis and simplified collection procedures, introducing a more progressive scale of tax assessment.

No less than individuals, companies felt the impact of the new approach to taxation. The regime corrected a number of anomalies that had grown up under inflation, by ordering firms to revalue their fixed assets and apply monetary correction[1] to this and other main items in their accounts. It raised basic company tax from 28 to 30 per cent and private enterprise, weakened by inflation, suffered under the burden of a tax policy that was beginning to be more efficiently enforced.

[1] Monetary correction: the adjustment of the face value of assets and liabilities so that their real value at the time of creation is maintained.

The regime's taxation policy was complemented by a wages and salary policy. It was laid down that the share of the wage-earners in the growth of the economy should be maintained and that disorderly increases likely to aggravate inflation should be prevented. Future increases should give the wage-earner the equivalent in purchasing power of the average real wages over the last two years, with the addition of an amount equivalent to the increase in productivity and a further amount corresponding to the estimate of the future rate of inflation.

During the Castello Branco administration, the control of wage and salary increases was strict and was exercised through the annual fixing of the minimum wage level and by the Ministry of Labour in its recommendation to the labour courts and those arbitrating between employers and employees. In the event, the regime proved unable to stem the rise in prices to the same extent that it held down wages; the result was an appreciable loss in the purchasing power of the wage-earners.

The period was one of belt-tightening, in which the wealthy had to begin paying their taxes, the middle classes felt the pinch and those in Brazil who lived not far from the subsistence level moved closer to it.

The unfulfilled expectations

With all the advantages of hindsight and armed with Roberto Campos' explanations, amongst others, it is easy to say that the authors of the PAEG were over-confident in their assumption that rapid and substantial progress could be made in reducing Brazil's headlong inflation; Campos himself seemed prepared, when out of office, to admit that the measures had been too drastic. Not surprisingly, the carefully devised programmes of the planners ran into difficulties that frustrated their aims.

A principal problem was to stem the flood of inflationary paper money and thereby moderate the rise in prices. The over-confidence lay in setting targets that overlooked the power of circumstances to produce large and unexpected obstacles. The planners, in drawing up the government's monetary budgets for 1964-6, set expansion rates of 70, 30 and 15 per cent for the money supply and said that, if the targets for growth were achieved, the rates of inflation for 1965 and 1966 should be of the order of 25 and 10 per cent respectively. In the event, the growth targets were not attained: the planners hoped to achieve a 6 per cent growth rate in both years but the actual results were

3.9 and 4.4 per cent. The rates of inflation for the two years, as measured by the increase in the cost of living, were 45 and 41 per cent.

The fight against inflation had begun badly when the regime awarded civil servants and the military larger pay increases than it could afford; after this error, however, the government got down to serious policy-making. It took steps that raised inflation initially but were essential to reduce government overspending, such as the removal of subsidies on imports of wheat, oil and newsprint. The consumer bore the burden of their elimination; this was 'corrective inflation' and it did not help to achieve good figures. Thus in 1964 the cost of living index for Rio de Janeiro rose by over 86 per cent, the highest figure in Brazilian history and the peak of the inflationary spiral.

In 1965 the authorities applied the brakes sharply, by tightening bank credit and controlling the minimum wage level. Business and industry soon began to feel the effects of a credit squeeze that bit deeply, especially in the second and third quarters, with an impact on the public's demand for consumer durables, notably domestic appliances and motor vehicles.

The policy of disinflation began to win results in slowing down the rate of price increases but evoked a chorus of complaint over the recession that now brought rising unemployment to São Paulo and protests from the National Confederation of Industry that the economic programme was encouraging stagnation and not stability. Campos and Bulhões pointed to a heartening 'reversal of expectations' on the future course of inflation, as the shops were forced to cut retail prices; but they also took relief measures to check the decline in production and demand, by means of excise tax reduction and special financing schemes to assist recession-hit industries. At the end of the third quarter of 1965 came recovery, with a gradual improvement in the level of employment in São Paulo, where in October Campos spoke to industry of the necessary and painful readjustment that it had just undergone, and stressed the signs of improvement in Brazil's balance of payments. By December, the rise in the cost of living had been almost halved, to 45 per cent, and in wholesale prices had fallen to under 30 per cent. This was progress by Brazilian standards, but not what the planners had hoped, and the future course of events was also to belie their expectations.

A marked decline in imports during 1965 by Brazilian industry, now struggling through a period of disinflation, led to an uncomfortably large surplus in the balance of trade and to large governmental outlays of cruzeiros to purchase exchange earned by the exporters. Large harvests further inflated government expenditure. One of the biggest coffee crops in Brazilian history, well above the original estimates, greatly increased payments to the coffee farmers, from whom the government was committed to buy quantities surplus to requirements for export and domestic consumption. The Bank of Brazil had to purchase additional agricultural surpluses in accordance with the policy of minimum prices. These obligations compelled the regime to issue large amounts of currency towards the end of 1965, stimulating a revival of inflation in the form of large price increases in early 1966, with repercussions on the rate of inflation for the year, which could not be held to less than 41 per cent.

The lessons of this disagreeable turn of events were taken to heart throughout 1966, when strict discipline was observed in the expansion of the money supply. Once again, however, the tightness of credit and the difficulties of many companies, particularly in maintaining working capital, led to a further weakening of the position of private enterprise. There were strong symptoms of recession in various sectors of industry at the end of 1966 and the beginning of 1967. Businessmen and industrialists complained that São Paulo was at a standstill and gave vent to their dislike of anti-inflation programmes. In fact, the worst was now over. The restraint exercised in 1966 was to bear fruit in making it possible to bring down the rate of inflation to 25 per cent in 1967. The sacrifices of three years of austerity and retrenchment had not been in vain.

A programme of reforms

Reducing the rate of inflation was a slow and painful process and proved to be a sure passport to unpopularity; Campos himself remarked that he needed a hide as tough as a Cuiabá Indian's to help him withstand the attacks, which came from all quarters: politicians, businessmen, shopkeepers and housewives. The Castello Branco regime was, however, able to tackle less ungrateful tasks; it was a period of unprecedented activity.

There was much to be done in the basic sectors of the economy. The private oil refineries expropriated by President Goulart had to be restored to their owners and the government-owned oil exploration and production monopoly, Petrobrás, had to be reorganized and managed on much more business-like lines. President Kubitschek had given a strong impetus to the development of the hydro-electric power resources and from 1964 the planners set in motion programmes to ensure their expansion. Brazil undertook, usually with international financing, large hydro-electric power projects to meet the future demands of industry and it also began to increase electricity supplies to the rural areas. The Castello Branco administration and those that followed it sought to organize investment and apply pricing policies that would generate funds for expansion.

There were serious difficulties in transport and communications, in which there was a legacy of backwardness and neglect. It was necessary to begin to rehabilitate and develop marine and rail transport, to accelerate the building of roads, to expand the telex and telephone networks and reconstruct the postal services.

These were domestic problems requiring long-term solutions. There were also international questions. Relations had to be restored with the World Bank, an important source of loan funds; decisions were needed on Brazil's foreign debt and the attitude to be adopted towards foreign capital.

There had been deficits in the balance of payments in many of the post-war years. In the 1950s, there was a steady build-up of the foreign debt, and in the '60s this became rapid, especially in short and medium-term obligations. In early 1964, the debt had reached the figure of 3,800 million dollars; there was a heavy concentration of repayments due in 1964-6, and there was no alternative for the Castello Branco administration but to seek help.

Brazil's negotiations with its creditors for the rescheduling of the debt repayments were marked by the initial success of the Paris Agreement signed in July 1964 and by the signing of bilateral agreements with the U.S.A., West Germany, France, the Netherlands, the United Kingdom, Italy, Switzerland and Japan. The Brazilians were at pains to convince their creditors of the seriousness of their intentions. After the Paris talks, their chief negotiator said that it was his government's evident determination to deal with the economic and financial problems that had made the negotiations successful. The task had been made easier by Brazil's removal of import subsidies, its adoption of a more realistic exchange policy, its efforts to reduce the budget deficit and, above all, by the proposed amendments to the foreign capital law, since the European creditors believed that the country's recovery would depend significantly on the co-operation of private foreign capital.

The overall negotiations were successfully concluded in 1965. The relative speed with which the whole process was completed was noteworthy; Brazil's creditors, some of whom had reason to be dissatisfied with its past record in this field, had made a contribution towards enhancing the new government's chances of success.

The law on foreign capital was signed by Castello in August 1964. It was a heavily amended version of legislation passed during the Goulart regime, which had regulated the application of foreign capital and the remittance of funds abroad; containing various restrictive clauses voted in by nationalist congressmen, the law had been a principal factor in drying up the inflow of foreign funds.

In his message to Congress introducing the bill, Castello said that foreign capital could contribute to the nation's growth by raising the rate of investment, strengthening the country's capacity to import, and increasing its stock of technology. Having recognized that foreign capital was desirable for Brazil, the Government had decided on a pragmatic policy with a single aim, to secure the greatest possible benefit. It was essential to remember that every restrictive regulation involved a reward and a price; the balance between the two required careful assessment. Any restriction on the free movement of foreign capital tended to discourage its entry, so that it was worth while only up to the point when economies in remittance compensated the loss of new capital. Following this point up in an appearance in the Chamber of Deputies, Campos spoke of the extent to which new foreign investment into Brazil had declined in recent years: entries in 1961 had amounted to 112m. dollars and had fallen successively to 71m. in 1962, 31m. in 1963, and nil in the first half of 1964.

In the event, the bill, which covered the whole field of entry and registration of foreign capital, reinvestment and remittance of profits, royalties and technical assistance payments, was amended in one important respect by Congress: profits and dividends remitted abroad (bearing a 25 per cent withholding tax) would be subject to a steeply progressive supplementary income tax, when the average of remittances during a three-year period exceeded 12 per cent of the capital and reinvested profits registered under the terms of the law. A restrictive system for foreign capital invested in producing luxury goods and services was also introduced. The law as a whole was certainly not a return to the liberal attitudes of the Kubitschek regime and was unlikely to stimulate a large inflow of private foreign capital. At least however, it reopened a door that had been slammed in 1962.

Conscious of the need to rebuild institutions and modernize administration, the Castello Branco regime turned to basic reforms, putting on the statute books measures that had dragged in and out of Congress for years without any prospect of being completed.

The most fruitful of these reforms were financial. The Banking Reform and the Capital Market laws were designed to help eliminate the financial chaos into which inflation had cast Brazil, and to provide a framework for the future. The former made an important innovation, by setting up a supervisory body, the National Monetary Council, to lay down and co-ordinate the policies to be followed by government in the monetary, credit, budgetary, fiscal and public debt sectors. It also established a Central Bank to execute the policies, issue the detailed regulations and conduct relations with the leading international and foreign financial agencies. The Capital Market law laid the foundations for the market's future development, assisting it to overcome the distortions imposed by inflation, and looked forward to more stable conditions when Brazil would have an organized stock-market, into which the public could put savings without being constantly defrauded of its money. Under this law, private investment banks, with a potentially significant role to play in financing development, began to be formed from 1966 onwards.

In addition to its income taxation measures, the regime began the task of bringing order to the tangled system of excise taxes and created two new instruments, a value-added tax on manufactured products paid to the federal government, and a goods circulation tax, the proceeds of which were shared by the state and municipal governments.

A housing programme was also launched. In a country where government agencies inspired little confidence, the National Housing Bank despite its early teething troubles, was one of the more successful initiatives, and made a positive contribution towards coping with the desperate backlog in house-building. It was able to increase its capital rapidly and raised money by placing its own commercial paper on the market; once its housing schemes had got under way, it provided a stimulus to the building industry and to the factories that supplied it with materials.

The Land Reform Law, passed in November 1964, had aims with which few Brazilians would openly quarrel: to change the existing system of land tenure and use, and to promote the better distribution of land in the interests of social justice and the increase of production. It was intended to favour the growth of a rural middle class of owners of small and medium-sized farms, to encourage agricultural production and to ensure adequate living standards for the rural worker. The principal instrument was to be progressive taxation to penalize absentee landlords and owners who flagrantly neglected the development of their land; the law included expropriation in the social interest, but this was to be a subsidiary tool of government action.

As was the custom in Brazil, the law set up new agencies, one to carry out a census and decide which regions most urgently needed land reform, another to organize technical assistance for the farmers. The effectiveness of this moderate law depended on these agencies working with drive and with full administrative support from the government; it also required the full enforcement and up-dating for inflation of the tax provisions. One of the agencies made a cadastral survey of rural properties during the Castello Branco regime. Under President Costa e Silva, who was far more ready to consider the interests of the landowners, governmental attention to and support for land reform seemed to vanish. The tax provisions were not fully up-dated, thus taking the teeth out of the law, and the agencies became discouraged.[1] In the event, action on the Land Reform law, with its 128 articles, was in inverse proportion to its length. It was left to President Médici in 1971, seven years after its enactment, to show that something might be done in the North and the North-East.

The neglect of this issue by yet more governments was perhaps symptomatic of the national disregard for rural life and for farming. 'The Japanese just plants, poor fellow', a city housewife remarked to the author, and her feeling of superiority was quite common. Brazilians are town and city-dwellers and over the countryside the shadow of the past hangs heavily. One authority writes that 'in the present day the influence of slavery still survives in social attitudes, in the landowners' refusal to

[1] A. Stepan, *The Military in Politics,* p. 236.

grant security to farm tenants, or rights of occupying landholdings to permanent labourers; and among the workers on the land it survives in the belief that agricultural labour is an indignity.'[1] There was no indigenous farming tradition in Brazil. 'Fire agriculture' or 'slash and burn' with use of the axe, machete and hoe and the burning of the vegetation, were the traditional means to prepare the soil for the seed; these were the methods first used by the indigenous Indians and the Brazilians for long went no further. Only the new European and Japanese farmers brought modern methods and techniques that stood in marked contrast to the type of agriculture practised by the landowner and the poor labourer without skills and resources.

It was refreshing to find that one of the most successful examples of settling farming communities in Brazil was given by a Scot. In June 1967 the municipal council of Londrina, situated some 230 miles into the interior of the state of Paraná, conferred an honorary citizenship on the late Lord Simon Lovat, recognizing the part that he had played in changing the face of Paraná.

To appreciate the scope of this distinguished Scot's contribution to the progress of this region, one must go back to 1924 when the Montague Commission, at the invitation of President Bernardes, went to Brazil to investigate the possibilities for British capital to take part in the country's development. As the Commission's expert on agriculture and forestry, Lovat travelled widely in Brazil, and his enthusiasm and pioneering instincts were kindled by the great potentialities of the fertile, densely forested virgin areas of Northern Paraná, lying below the border with the state of São Paulo. Returning to London, Lovat won the support of a group of City financiers with whom he set up the Brazil Plantations Syndicate, with a capital of £200,000, and an initial plan for the growing of cotton and the forming of settlements. A British manager for the Brazilian operations was brought in from the Sudan.

Lovat's bid to build up cotton production in Northern Paraná was frustrated by a slump in world prices, but this did not prevent the venture from going forward; a new company was formed with increased capital, Paraná Plantations Ltd., out of which grew a Brazilian subsidiary, the North Paraná Land Company. Within five years, the Company acquired a concession of some three million acres and a controlling share in a small

[1] D. Warriner, *Land Reform in Principle and Practice,* p. 271.

Sâo Paulo-Paraná railway, pushing its railhead forward in the concession area to a small settlement of wooden huts that, at the suggestion of one of Lovat's Brazilian associates, was christened Londrina in recognition of the Company's London connections.

During these and subsequent years and despite the problems caused by the world-wide depression of the early 1930s a carefully planned settlement scheme, based on the encouragement of the small farmer, was set in motion and progressively expanded. Facing the encroachments of claim-jumpers and land-grabbers, the Company placed the maximum emphasis on security of tenure for the settlers, even when this might involve its paying twice for the same piece of land. With this security as a stabilizing force and a steady influx of European, Japanese and Brazilian immigrants, lured by the rich red soil that is among the most fertile in the world, Northern Paraná went ahead with the production of timber, cereals and coffee as well as cattle-raising.

During the Second World War, suffering a fate similar to that of many British investments overseas, the Land Company passed to Brazilian owners, who however continued its policies and diversified into other activities. Today Northern Paraná, part of a fast-developing state, is a region of prosperity, the world's foremost coffee producing area with its capital in Londrina, now a thriving municipality of nearly 230,000 people, a 'little London' given its start in life by Scottish initiative.

5 Politics and Development: The Military Role

Military interventions in political life, such as took place from 1930 to 1964, were part of a process that had its antecedents in Brazilian history: they were indeed a feature of politics from the 1880s onwards.

From the day when the Republicans and the Army, backed by the Church, joined to expel the Emperor Dom Pedro II in 1889 and end the monarchy, the military made their voice increasingly heard in the affairs of the country. They had been encouraged to assert themselves by the army's earlier successes in consolidating the nation's frontiers, particularly in the war against Paraguay from 1865-70, and they developed a self-confidence that contributed to the emergence of a military elite and to its assumption of a role in national politics.[1]

The events of 1889 contributed to this. In deposing the Emperor, who had ruled with a parliamentary system, the politicians and the military had removed a vital element, the 'moderating power', for the Emperor had always arbitrated the rotation of the parties in power and retained the prerogative of limiting the length of their stay.[2] His departure left a power vacuum, and there were early signs that it would be filled by the armed forces. Under the Republic, the first two Presidents, Deodoro da Fonseca and Floriano Peixoto, were from the army. Thereafter, with the exception of a relapse into military-backed government before the First World War, civilians assumed the Presidency, but the role of the armed forces as a potential balancing factor in politics had already begun to take root.

The history of the time shows that, from the outset, there was tension between civilians and soldiers over the exercise of power, but that the politicians frequently encouraged the military to use it. Thus, amid the vicissitudes of political life under the Republic, when the military were involved in more than one crisis, the

[1] A. Marshall, *Brazil,* p. 89.

[2] J. M. Bello, *A History of Modern Brazil,* pp. 23-4.

politicians were quite ready to call them in when they thought it would be to their own advantage, while the soldiers, as was for example later shown in the case of the Lieutenants' revolts, were ready actively to propagate their own ideas of what should be done to resolve the problems of Brazil.

The assignment of a political role to the military took shape in the successive constitutions of the Republic. Three of the four constitutions passed between 1892 and 1946 included clauses that, if they did not specifically mention the idea of a moderating power, implied that the military should exercise one. The evidence indicates that they were included because the civilian politicians wanted them to be, despite initial resistance by the armed forces, President Fonseca himself having strongly opposed adoption of one of these clauses on the grounds that it would be bad for military discipline.[1]

The gist of them was that the armed forces were responsible for defending the fatherland, and for guaranteeing the constitutional powers and law and order. They were defined as permanent national institutions, organized on the basis of hierarchy and discipline, under the supreme command of the President of the Republic and within the limits of the law. The first of these provisions in effect gave the armed forces ultimate powers to intervene in the event of crises in the relations between the Executive, the Legislature and Judiciary, or even of any acute national crisis. The second discouraged them from deposing the President, who was their supreme commander under the constitution, but also implied that their obedience to him depended on the lawfulness of his actions. In practice therefore, they had ultimate responsibility for checking the actions of the Executive.

With the passage of time came the consolidation of the role of the military as arbiters within the political system, as referees in the game of Brazilian politics, able to blow the whistle for fouls, to send players off or order a replay. The nature of this role and its effect upon the formation of opinion in the officer corps have been summed up as follows:

> Historically, civilians who form the politically relevant strata of Brazilian society have always attempted to use the military to further their own political goals. Coupled with the diversity and openness of the Brazilian military institution, this has

[1] Alfred Stepan, *The Military in Politics,* pp. 75-77.

meant that military officers have always been highly politicized. A further consequence of the internal diversity of the military and persistent attempts by civilian groups to co-opt military officers into politics is that the military is never unified in its political beliefs and ideology, but is normally reflective to some degree of the broad range of civilian opinion.[1]

Fulfilling a political role, the armed forces, led by the army as the senior service, were deeply involved in the events of the twentieth century. During the period from 1930 to 1964, for example, they were called on by various civilian groups, or on their own initiative decided, to support new political movements (1930), to back a move to autocratic government (1938), to guarantee the holding of free elections (1945), to ensure the legal transfer of power (1955) and to secure the resignation of the President or, finally, to depose him (1945, 1954 and 1964).

In exercising a moderating power and taking political action, they had to measure the strength of public opinion and to establish their own consensus, since their political interventions, which were often a source of disagreement among the officer corps, were liable to place severe strains upon their unity. Maintenance of unity within their ranks was therefore a primary consideration and political action could be either abandoned or frustrated in its absence, or delayed until the necessary degree of unity had been achieved. This could at times be a complicated matter. There were large military concentrations in the cities in which the four main army commands were located—Rio, São Paulo, Pôrto Alegre and Recife—but the three services were scattered over a huge territory. This dispersion, with the responsibility borne by unit commanders and their degree of autonomy, had important effects in potentially reducing the powers of control of top commanders. In times of crisis, when political decisions were called for and unity of purpose was necessary, it was essential for the generals to have their subordinates behind them, especially if the latter commanded sizeable bodies of troops. This situation enabled the middle-ranking officers, if they felt strongly on some important political issue, to exert pressure on the senior officers.[2]

[1] Ibid, p 67.
[2] Ibid, p. 28.

As professional bodies, the armed forces enjoyed a stronger tradition from the days of the Duke of Caxias, an outstanding military leader of the nineteenth century, who was commander-in-chief in the war against Paraguay and was considered to be the father of the Army for his work in reorganizing it and making it a disciplined force.[1] Even today, in everyday conversation, a Brazilian may quote him as an example of hard work, while Caxias' interest in organization and training had some lasting effects. The army today has some of the best educational and training facilities in the country. The network of military schools, which take boys from the age of 13, the Military Academy at Agulhas Negras (the Brazilian counterpart of Sandhurst or West Point), requiring the candidate to pass a competitive entry examination and giving him a university level education, the technical standards of bodies like the Institute of Military Engineering and the system of regular refresher and specialized courses for officers, all provide a competitive framework that is unfortunately seldom surpassed in the civilian sector. Like armies elsewhere, the Brazilian army subjects its officer cadres to a process of change and renewal, through its system of promotions and by ensuring that in the senior ranks the regulations on compulsory retirement are rigorously enforced.

Of the three services, the navy appears to draw its officers from the higher social levels and the air force broadly follows the pattern of the army. Army officers come predominantly from the middle class and, in small degree, from the lower class, a father to son tradition being especially strong, while a good number of officers come from families of civil servants, merchants and tradesmen; the sons of wealthy, upper-class families seldom enter the army, which does not offer high rates of pay.[2]

Officers, as well as other ranks, generally come from the cities, many from Rio, where there is a large military garrison and a number of military institutions, but few from São Paulo, which offers the possibility of much more lucrative careers in business and industry. Rio Grande do Sul, with its military tradition as a frontier area, its large numbers of settlers of German origin, and its military school at Pôrto Alegre, provides a number of officers out of proportion to its population. However, the country-

[1] A. Marshall, *Brazil*, p. 219.

[2] See A. Stepan, *The Military in Politics*, pp. 30-56.

wide schools system does enable men from the poorer states of the North, the North-East or the Centre-West to enter the service. Thus Marshal Dutra, who became President of Brazil, was the son of a barber from Mato Grosso.

In terms of numbers, the army is the largest of the services, even though many units are below strength. Total figures for the armed forces in 1968 were estimated at 234,000, with over two thirds of the number in the army, which had over 13,000 career officers.[1] There was therefore no doubt of the role of the army as the senior service. Foreign observers did not see it as modern in its equipment, the country's financial problems in the 1950s and '60s having brought investment in this sector down to a very low level. The Brazilians had been for some years tired of getting, admittedly for practically nothing, obsolete U.S. equipment used in the Second World War and were anxious to re-equip with modern weapons, buying from the sources best suited to their needs and developing the capacity of Brazilian industry to manufacture equipment and materials.

In the years following the coup of March 31st 1964, during which three military Presidents took office, the organizational structure of the military assumed increasing importance inasmuch as political power was now in their hands. At the apex of the pyramid was the President, who had his own military household run by a general, whose task was to maintain contact with the military. In second place was the Minister for the Army, who was able to represent to the President happenings and opinions in his service, in the same way as the Navy and Air Force Ministers did for theirs. Next in the hierarchy were the four-star generals commanding the four armies. The Army Minister and chief of staff, the army commanders and the five generals running substantive departments in the Ministry, constituted the army high command, which met in times of crisis.

Beneath the army commanders, were the commanders of the 12 military regions (including two important ones located at Brasília and in Amazonas) into which the commands were subdivided. These men had major responsibilities for maintaining law and order and keeping the regime informed; they and the unit commanders were the watch-dogs of the Movement of

[1] Ibid, p. 26.

March 1964, with considerable local prestige and responsibilities.[1]

During the period of military rule, officers were increasingly to be found in governmental administrative positions. Under the rule included by Castello in the 1967 Constitution and apparently intended to inhibit 'empire-building' by the military, an officer assuming a permanent post in the public service must after two years opt either to return to active service or, if he wished to remain in the post, to go on the reserve list.

Civilians as a whole were hardly likely to welcome the greater military presence in government, nor were they always complimentary about the mentality of the soldiers. Talk to middle-class Brazilians about them and some would use the word 'bitolado', explaining it with a two-handed gesture suggesting blinkers and indicating that the men in uniform thought within narrow, well-defined limits.

The search for an elite

Carlos Lacerda, journalist, administrator and a 'maverick' among Brazilian political leaders, who was state governor of Guanabara in the 1960s, once told a group of foreign correspondents in Rio that Brazil's problems could be summed up in one : the lack of an elite organized and ready to govern, and that one of the principal factors contributing to this deficiency was the long period of the Vargas regime, when Brazil failed to develop and train leaders for the future.[2]

The thesis was convincing. A foreign observer was tempted to attribute the lack principally to the nation-wide deficiencies in education. Lacerda's argument seemed to be borne out by other missing links—the inability of the political parties to present and follow imaginative, valid national programmes, the apparent lack of institutions taking a broad, coherent view of the country's problems and training people to understand them. With the exception of the Getúlio Vargas Foundation, a competent technical body, there seemed to be a dearth of such national institutions. Under President Kubitschek, one such body, the

[1] It is tempting to recall the Cromwellian division of England and Wales into eleven districts in 1655, when the Major-Generals were given the function of police and public order, the collection of special taxes and the strict enforcement of Puritan morality.

[2] Lacerda was later deprived of his political rights by the Costa e Silva regime.

Higher Institute of Brazilian Studies (ISEB), had made a promising start as a civilian centre for research and teaching on the national development problems. It published 'a stream of books and lectures offering a rationale for industrialization and explaining the cause and effect of under-development in every sector of the country's society and economy. The hundreds of younger Brazilians who attended the one-year Course at the Institute were profoundly influenced by the developmentalist mystique'.[1] The ISEB, however, threw away its initial impetus and success in quarrels between moderates and extreme leftists; it was closed down in 1964.

It is a sad reflection on the strength and durability of Brazil's civilian institutions that, in order to find an institution that lasted and remained organized, one has to turn to the armed forces, which themselves set up a centre to train an elite in the study and analysis of Brazilian problems.

This centre, the Escola Superior de Guerra (ESG), or War College, could be considered as a further agency to train the military. It was so, but became more than this; despite its establishment within, and control by, the armed forces, it was also to be open substantially to civilians, acquiring a broader national significance. A training centre and debating forum, the ESG, through its permanent staff, developed a doctrine and methods of analysis that influenced the civilians that passed through it and, most especially, a part of the Brazilian officer corps, which looked to the ESG as its own research centre and laboratory of ideas.

In the years preceding the coup of 1964, the ESG helped to strengthen the middle class reaction against the Left and against the general conduct of government, becoming a rallying point for those opposed to the Goulart regime. Its existence probably persuaded some officers that the military had a valid approach for dealing with the national problems and a programme to develop the country, and to this extent strengthened their resolve to assume full powers in 1964. Thus, from April 1964, the Movement was, in part, to look for its ideology to the ESG, with which Castello himself had been closely connected as an instructor and director of studies.[2]

[1] T. E. S. Skidmore, *Politics in Brazil 1930-64*, pp. 170, 180.

[2] The group of officers led by Castello and associated with the ESG acquired the nickname of the 'Sorbonne group'.

The ESG's origins go back to 1948 when President Dutra told the general staff to set it up, with the initial task of giving a staff course to senior officers of the three services. A further order in 1949, however, set up under the same roof an 'institute of higher studies for the planning and control of the national security.' In its beginnings, it owed much to the co-operation between the Brazilian and U.S. armies, strengthened by the presence of the Brazilian expeditionary force in the American Fifth Army during the war in Italy. The Americans gave assistance in the early organization of the ESG and today maintain a liaison officer within the College. In the preparatory phase, Brazilian staff officers went to the U.S.A. to report on the working of the U.S. National War College and an American mission visited Brazil to advise.

The Brazilians considered that there could be no question of making the ESG a replica of the American counterpart. General Cordeiro de Farias, who had commanded the Brazilian artillery in Italy and was the ESG's first commandant, took the three officers of the American mission on an extensive trip round Brazil and, not surprisingly, this convinced the Americans that it did not make sense to copy the U.S. model.[1] The name, borrowed from the American counterpart, remained but did not fully reflect the activities of the College, which came to be as much concerned with the development of the national potential in peacetime as with training officers in the practice of war.

Today, in its colonial-style building at the foot of the 'sugar-loaf' mountain that overlooks the bay of Rio de Janeiro, the ESG looks back on more than two decades as a school for military and civilians. By early 1970 it had graduated 1,250 military and over 800 civilians, concentrating its activities in three courses. One of these was strictly military, an armed forces command and general staff course attended by 30 officers from the three services. Another was the intelligence course, which was limited to 18 civilians and officers and came into full operation only in 1965, after the creation of the National Information Service. Finally, the ESG ran a higher war course held since its foundation, the objectives of which were to prepare civilians and military for the exercise of leadership and advisory functions in agencies responsible for the formulation, development and execution of a national security policy.

[1] From comments made to the author by the now Marshal Cordeiro de Farias in Rio.

This last course was to provide the framework in which Brazilians could work together and establish methods for the solution of the national problems; in a lecture on the ESG given at São Paulo in May 1970, General Augusto Fragoso, then the College's commandant, said that it acted as a powerful and fruitful instrument of cultural communion between civilians and military. The College brought together on a full-time basis (some with high-level jobs were permitted part-time working) from 80 to 90 persons for a ten months higher war course covering a very broad range of Brazilian political, economic, financial and social problems, in their national and international aspects.[1] Senior officers from the three services, lieutenant-colonels and above, provided about a third of the course members, while the remainder were lawyers, diplomats, engineers, doctors, economists and businessmen, with the civil servant element probably the most numerous. Civilians attending had to be over 35 and university graduates. These men were nominated for the course by ministries, confederations of industry, institutes of engineering or scientific institutes, amongst others.

Built round the concepts of national security and development, a typical course included field trips, usually to Brazil's most under-developed areas. The military regime made sure that it had the highest level teaching available. The opening lecture of the course was given by the President of the Republic, who usually made an important statement of national policy. Generally, the lectures were given by cabinet ministers and leading national authorities and experts while foreign personalities, including ambassadors, were also invited to address the course (the former W. German Chancellor, Ludwig Ehrhard, was an example).

The ultimate responsibility for the direction of the ESG lay with the three military ministries and the Foreign Office, which provided by rotation the men to fill the top posts on the staff of the College. Gen. Fragoso liked to define it as an institute of higher studies and a permanent research centre, 'a school without teachers and without pupils', by which he meant that a lecturer might later become a course member and that the latter might subsequently address courses as a lecturer.

The organization of the three courses was supported by a per-

[1] For example, a lecture attended by the author at the ESG was concerned with the national policy for the welfare of the minor.

manent staff, including a department of studies under a general, which provided the courses with the necessary means for the development and co-ordination of their curricula and assured unity of doctrine. While the ESG disclaimed any direct involvement in the affairs of government after 1964, its permanent staff was probably consulted by the military-backed regimes for its views on particular problems. President Médici, in an address at the ESG in March 1970, recommended that it play an increasingly active part.

The training of some 2,000 military and civilians in a knowledge of political, economic and social affairs would normally, in a country as large as Brazil, be considered a useful contribution, but hardly on a large enough scale to make a dent in the country's problems. The ESG, however, sought to spread the message through its Graduates Association, which was the vehicle by which the ESG and its graduates remained in contact and which, with a nationwide network of delegates and a permanent staff of lecturers, undertook the task of disseminating the doctrine and ideas of the College throughout Brazil. In 1969, in cities and towns of all the main regions of Brazil, it held courses on national security and development, in which over 2,100 persons took part and received diplomas. These courses followed in a shortened form the pattern of those given in the ESG. The 1970 programme stepped up the number of courses and covered most of the state capitals in the North-East. Increasing attention was given by the Association to bringing the message to opinion leaders throughout the Brazilian interior.

The operation received official support. Each ministry of the Médici government, which took office in October 1969, had a department of security and information headed by an Association member; seven cabinet ministers were graduates. Indeed, the ESG and its Graduates Association now provided a new potential elite for the Movement of March 1964, which through them hoped to win the support of opinion leaders all over the country. By 1970 the demand for ESG-type training had risen substantially and there was talk of setting up an expanded operation, this time in São Paulo, the industrial heart of the country.

An ideology for development?

An institute of higher studies and a research centre, the ESG developed ideas that from 1964 were constantly mentioned in the public statements of several of the Movement's leaders. Foremost among these ideas were 'national security' and 'permanent national objectives', basic elements in the Movement's political attitudes and development policies, even if the doctrine, of which they formed part, was certainly not endorsed by everyone in the officer corps.[1]

For a long time in Brazil, national security was considered from the viewpoint of the country's defence against attack from abroad. In the liberal constitution of 1946, which was shattered by the Institutional Acts and finally replaced by Castello's constitution of 1967, this was the approach adopted. The President headed a National Security Council, including the civilian cabinet ministers, the three military ministers and the chiefs of staff of the three services, which was to study defence problems and assist him in times of national crisis. The Movement of 1964 enhanced the importance of the Council but swept away this view of national security, replacing it with a doctrine of which the keynote was internal security, the defence of the national institutions, the preservation of development and of political stability. The threat of external aggression yielded first place to the danger of attacks from within, based on ideological infiltration, subversion and guerrilla movements that might be supported from abroad.

In their development aspects, these ideas were broadly expressed as follows: the national security was a function of the overall potential of the nation rather than of its military potential and therefore, in order to achieve security, the general development of the nation must be fostered. It was the duty of those responsible for security—the armed forces—to watch over the development of the national potential. Brazil possessed the basic elements in area, population and natural resources needed to become a great power, but its development had been held up by various obstacles; these must be removed and there must be an acceleration of the rate of development. Energies must be harnessed and an elite must be formed to undertake the task of building up the nation. The resources existed among the civilians and military, but they lacked the habit of working together. They must be brought together to acquire a common method of analysis and interpretation of the factors involved in the solution of Brazilian

[1] In the law of March 1967, the national security was defined as 'the guarantee of the achievement of the national objectives against internal or external opposition'.

problems. An atmosphere of understanding must be created among the national groups and the method should be applied by all responsible civilian and military bodies.

Castello presented these ideas in a more elaborate form in an address on security and development given at the ESG in March 1967, on the eve of the handing over of power to President Costa e Silva. Genuine security pre-supposed a process of balanced economic and social development. In the economic sense, a country's industry and level of technology ultimately determined its military power. Socially speaking, even a satisfactory level of economic development, if accompanied by excessive concentration of wealth and growing social inequalities, led to tension and strife that would prevent the institutions from working properly and would compromise development and security, Castello declared. Economic and social development required a minimum of stability, not only of the political institutions that determined the level of efficiency of public investments, but also of the economic and legal institutions that guaranteed contracts and property rights and determined the level and efficiency of private investments.

In the emphasis that it placed on development and on the planning of governmental action, the ESG provided a meeting-ground for the alliance of military and technocrats that was a predominant feature of Brazilian governments after 1964. The consummation of this alliance was no accident, since the leading technocrats, including such men as Roberto Campos, regularly addressed the courses at the ESG and contributed to the formation of opinion among the military and civilians attending them.[1] In this type of alliance, which some of the military wished to use as an instrument for modernization and development, there was no room for the traditional political classes.

In view of the diversity of opinion among Brazilian officers, it was not surprising that the Movement of March 1964 lacked a comprehensive, agreed statement of its political aims. One exposition of a national policy, representative of a part of the officer corps, was, however, worthy of study. In his 'Essay on the political doctrine of the revolution', General Meira Mattos, who as a colonel was a member of Castello's military household and the regime's 'trouble-shooter', said that the Movement's doctrine was based on nine national objectives, to be achieved by the

[1] Alfred Stepan, *The Military in Politics*, p. 218 (footnote).

execution of a national policy and the application of national power. The achievement of five of these presented the greatest challenge: national integration, national prosperity, democracy, the preservation of the moral and spiritual values of the nation and social peace. Priority was assigned to the first two. 'In order to have any right to a vocation for greatness, we must prove our ability as a revolution to achieve, at all costs and in the short term, the two objectives on which the revolution's development policy is based' the general said. The progress gained in the achievement of the five objectives would help to strengthen and consolidate those objectives that, having already been won, must be preserved: independence, sovereignty, territorial integrity, and international prestige.

It was on the development policy that Brazil depended to break down the barriers to progress and the General said that this would not be achieved without a cohesive, disciplined elite, conscious of the effort and sacrifices required. It must be a modern elite, formed from enlightened politicians, competent specialists and skilled technicians, with a missionary spirit and imbued with the principles of a revolutionary doctrine based on authority, austerity, administrative efficiency, dynamic policies, productivity, freedom with responsibility, private enterprise, social peace and respect for the dignity of the human person. When the country's economic weakness had been overcome, it would possess a national power sufficient to achieve its destiny of greatness.

These ideas were similar to those put forward by General Golbery, the intellectual of the Movement, who played a leading part in the conspiracy that led to the coup of 1964 and was later appointed the first head of the national information service. Golbery was an exponent of geopolitics,[1] setting out a strategy for the integration of the country and showing the ways to overcome the geographical obstacles to its development.[2] Equally, he was a spokesman for the doctrine of national security current at the War College.

Liberal civilian opinion, of which the leading São Paulo daily *O Estado* was an example, did not like the doctrine. That

[1] Geopolitics: the politics of a country as determined by its geographical position.

[2] See Oliveiros S. Ferreira, 'Politica castrense', in *Aportes,* Paris, April 1969.

some officers, including the more nationalist, did not accept the outlook and ideology associated with the College, was also apparent, but the extent of opposition was difficult to assess. The administration that followed Castello's, that of President Costa e Silva, was less concerned with, and apparently much less convinced by, these ideas.

6 Costa e Silva: Political Slump and Economic Recovery

In contrast to Castello, a 'soldier's professor,' Marshal Costa e Silva who took over the Presidency in March 1967, was a conventional soldier. In personality, they also differed. Castello sometimes kept people at a distance, but Costa e Silva, in this respect typically Gaúcho[1], was sociable, enjoying his food and his glass of whisky, a game of poker with his friends or a visit to the racecourse. He was an uncomplicated, kindly man, devoted to his family, and his origins were plain enough: he was born in Taquari, a small town in Rio Grande do Sul, of a family of small tradespeople who had little money. He was, however, an outstanding pupil at the military schools and colleges.

The qualities that made him a good soldier were not necessarily those of a good President, nor were some of his other virtues. His friendliness and informality, for instance, did not give him the aura that his fellow-countrymen liked a President to have: to receive a group of students in his shirt-sleeves at the palace in Brasília was not what Brazilians expected of a President, and only created an impression that he was too plebeian for the job. In the Presidency he lacked the bureaucratic virtues, the ability to organize his time methodically, and this hindered him in the work of directing a team of ministers and assistants.

Although he was over 64 when he became President, he was prodigal, even careless, of his time and energy—witness the late hours that he kept chatting with friends and his initiative in taking the government out to the capitals of various states, an exacting routine for a man of his age. In office he was a fatherly chairman of the board rather than a chief executive, a man who was at the head of affairs but not controlling them. Facing a task as difficult as that of his predecessor, he was more sensitive to criticism and more emotional in his reactions than Castello

[1] Gaúcho: a native of the state of Rio Grande do Sul.

and the physical and mental burdens of office finally proved too much for his health.

When he assumed the Presidency, Brazil was ready for a relaxation of its mood after three years of austerity, belt-tightening and listening to home truths under the Castello Branco regime. Among the public there was a hope of better times while politicians and businessmen were looking forward to concessions. The original basis of support for the Movement of March 1964 had been heavily eroded. Politicians who had backed it wavered when it became clear that the military intended to retain full powers indefinitely; other politicians who had sat on the fence were antagonized by their loss of status and the elimination of their powers of patronage. Industrialists were often perplexed by the rigours of disinflation, and even some of the senior generals had become alienated. Under these circumstances, the more expansive personality of President Costa e Silva—who expressed his wish to 'humanize the revolution'—the expiry of the Institutional Acts and the entry into force of the new constitution, all contributed to a reduction of tensions.

The new cabinet, which included a number of military men, was a completely new team, heterogeneous and less cohesive than its predecessor. General Lyra Tavares became Minister of the Army and Magalhães Pinto was appointed Foreign Minister to implement a more independent foreign policy and a 'diplomacy of prosperity'. A strong nationalist line was represented by General Albuquerque Lima, the Minister of the Interior responsible for the regional development agencies. In the absence of effective political leadership by the President, the tendency developed for Ministers to go their own way, and in due course some began to foster actively their own Presidential aspirations, a number of potential candidates having appeared within a year of the regime taking office.

There were shifts in policy and a change in the political climate. Costa e Silva did not share the more international outlook of Castello; he had not served with the army in Italy nor did he have close associations with the War College. The new regime changed course in foreign affairs, on the grounds that the country was ready to reassert its national identity and modify a policy considered by some to have been too friendly to the U.S.A. At home, official statements that with some exceptions those deprived of their political rights could return (provided that they were ready to take any legal consequences), contributed to a feeling of détente that for the moment disarmed opposition. The President was ready to establish a dialogue with the various sectors of opinion and, in a bid to regain popular support for the Movement, he and his Labour Minister, Jarbas Passarinho, made conciliatory overtures to the working classes, promising more constructive treatment in the form of a relaxation of the strict wages policy. By placing on the universities the onus of finding space for the large numbers of unmatriculated students, the regime sought to avoid a worsening of relations with students generally.

In April 1967, ex-President Kubitschek had again returned to Brazil, with the apparent intention of remaining. It was reported that Carlos Lacerda might be brought back into the fold, thus reinforcing the tendency of the regime to move towards a government of national union, which would have been in keeping with the paternalistic outlook of the President.[1] There was increasing support amongst the politicians for the revision of the new constitution and the national security and press laws.

It was not long, however, before the military reacted against any idea that concessions be made to the political classes. In the early months of the new regime, some of the military leaders spoke strongly against any revision of measures taken under the Institutional Acts to deprive the 'subversive' and 'corrupt' of their political rights. These declarations were backed up by reported comment by the President that any desire to grant amnesty or revise the main 'revolutionary' legislation was premature. There was a stiffening of military attitudes.

At an early stage the country became aware that it was being run with looser reins. For some Cariocas[2], it was no longer a hard but a soft dictatorship (a 'ditamole' not a 'ditadura'). São Paulo taxi-drivers commented that the President lacked drive ('não tem pulso'), drawing unfavourable comparisons with the city's new mayor, Brigadier Faria Lima, already being praised as 'a great Brazilian' and undertaking with rough determination the task of rebuilding and reorganizing the city.

As a President whose support was essentially military, but who was bound to be involved in relations with the politicians, Marshal Costa e Silva found difficulty in playing a dynamic role

[1] Lacerda in fact later tried, in association with ex-Presidents Kubitschek and Goulart, two of his former political enemies, to set up a 'broad front' of opposition to the regime.

[2] Carioca : a citizen of Rio de Janeiro.

in his relations with Congress. From the beginning it seemed that the President preferred, as far as possible, to devote himself to the tasks of administration, with the principal objective of consolidating the work of his predecessor. He sought to govern from Brasília and was successful in improving the regime's image; by transferring the government to São Paulo, Recife and Belo Horizonte for short spells, he helped to bring the regime closer to the people and to increase understanding of regional problems. As President he was less active than Castello in conducting relations with the official party, the Arena, which contained a wide assortment of political opinions and was not a cohesive body. The opposition, in the form of the Movimento Democrático Brasileiro, was scarcely more organized.

The Death of Castello

After handing over the Presidency to his successor, Castello had travelled to Europe, visiting the birthplace of his ancestors in Portugal. On returning to Brazil, he went back to his home state of Ceará to visit familiar places and look up old friends, journeying out to Quixadá, some 100 miles in the interior, to stay at the country house of the authoress Raquel de Queiroz. On the morning of July 18th Castello travelled back from Quixadá with his brother Cândido in a Piper Aztec belonging to the Ceará state government. As the plane came in to land at Fortaleza, it collided with a jet trainer aircraft of the Air Force, flying in a four-plane formation on a routine flight. The jet lost only a wing tank and was able to land, but Castello's plane, its controls shattered, plummeted down, killing him and his brother, as well as other members of his party.[1]

When the news reached the Centre-South, some voiced suspicions that Castello's death had been contrived—by the 'powerful interests' to which ordinary Brazilians sometimes attribute the occurrence of disaster. The findings of the official inquiry were clear, however. Neither pilot had disobeyed the regulations or was otherwise to blame; the fault lay in the lack of a strictly controlled, separate air space for the take-off and landing of the fighter aircraft.

With the abrupt removal from the political scene of a strong

[1] José Wamberto, *Castello Branco, Revolução e Democracia,* Rio de Janeiro, 1970, pp. 155-7.

leader, who still had much to contribute to his country's progress, part of the backbone went out of the Movement of March 1964. Castello had been in many respects a good President and in his integrity and dedication to his office had shown outstanding qualities. His departure substantially altered the political climate; leadership of the military now polarized around Costa e Silva, the group of officers identified with Castello and the War College being without a prominent leader. The new President's position was for the moment unchallenged.

The crisis build-up: the urban guerrilla movement

The political calm that characterized the early months of the Costa e Silva regime did not last; from the end of 1967 a threefold challenge developed, of which the strongest manifestation came from the revolutionary Left.[1]

The speed of the military intervention on March 31st 1964 had caught the Brazilian Communist movement off balance, striking a blow at the process of infiltration undertaken by the party. For some Communists, the failure of the Soviet-line policies of the 'establishment', headed by the ageing Luís Carlos Prestes, was now obvious. In 1962 those following the Chinese line had warned that the peaceful road to revolution was barred by the ruling classes and that, without abandoning all the forms of legal struggle, the people should prepare themselves for a non-peaceful solution.[2]

After the military coup of 1964 there was an increasing number of party members ready to reject Prestes' leadership and turn to Cuba as their model for action. The split in the party ranks widened and could no longer be repaired. In 1966 student cells in the Rio universities rejected the policy advocated by the Central Committee, while a growing faction, led by Mário Alves and Carlos Marighela, called for an armed struggle as the only means to gain power. Events abroad strengthened their hand. The Tricontinental conference of 1966, attended by Communist representatives from Asia, Africa and Latin America, as well as the conference of the Organization of Latin American Solidarity

[1] For purposes of cohesion, the events in this section cover the Presidencies of Costa e Silva and Médici, as well as the interregnum.

[2] Carlos Marighela: Conrad Detrez (ed.), *Pour la libération du Brésil,* Paris, published jointly by Aubier-Montaigne and 22 publishers, 1970, p. 30.

(OLAS) at Havana in August 1967, offered fresh encouragement to those wishing to take up arms. 'Che' Guevara had called for 'two, three, several Vietnams' in Latin America and the final proclamation of the OLAS conference ended with the slogan that it was 'the duty of every revolutionary to make the revolution'.

Marighela had already resigned from the party executive in 1966 and his defiant attendance at the OLAS meeting marked his final breach with the 'establishment'; it was followed by his call to unite the forces of the coming revolution, the vanguard of which was to be the guerrilla movement. Prestes and his supporters refused to be persuaded and expelled Marighela from the party, but by the end of 1967 the new groups of left-wing revolutionaries, under Marighela's general inspiration, were beginning to organize in Brazil and prepare for the struggle.

He was one of those Brazilian mixtures, the son of an Italian immigrant and a negress, a Baiano[1] who said that he was a grandson of slaves. His whole adult life was spent in the Communist party, in which he was militant from the age of 16; he spent a few years at the university studying to be an engineer but never graduated and devoted his whole career to the party. He was a member of its 'suicide squad', well known for his reckless courage, a born agitator, who was even briefly elected to Congress but, apart from a few years' study trip to Communist China, spent much of his life in underground activities all over Brazil. He worked for many years to maintain unity but was a man of action and finally rejected what he considered was a party given over to bureaucracy.

Marighela saw his country as having been for several years in a permanent political crisis.[2] This must be turned into an armed conflict by unleashing in the cities and in the country so many armed actions that those in power would be obliged to transform the political situation of the country into a military one. The masses would then be antagonized and would revolt against the regime's police and army as being responsible for this situation. The alliance of the masses and of its guerrilla vanguard would lead to the destruction of the administrative and military apparatus of the state and to the seizure of power, Marighela declared. This would be achieved in a three-stage campaign: the prepara-

[1] Baiano: a native of the state of Bahia.
[2] Ibid, p. 35.

tion and organization of guerrilla groups, the initiation and establishment of guerrilla activities, and their further development into a war of movement. It was typical of his reckless courage that he drew up this plan only a few days after 'Che' Guevara's death, following the failure of 'Che's' attempt to build up guerrilla activity in Bolivia.

In 1969 Marighela issued a document that illuminated the whole course of terrorist activities in Brazil, the 'Mini-manual of the Urban Guerrilla', in which he drew on some eighteen months of practical experience.[1] A blueprint for civil war and a bloodbath, its objective was to help dismantle and destroy the existing economic, political and social system in Brazil, which would be replaced by an entirely new political and social structure, with the people armed and in power.

Marighela spelled out the targets for guerrilla attack. The broad objective was to shake the foundations of the new Brazil, 'of the triangular region sustaining the Brazilian state system and American domination of Brazil, whose vertices are Rio, São Paulo and Belo Horizonte and whose base is the Rio-São Paulo axis, where is located the giant complex holding all powers of decision in the country'.[2] The aim was to weaken the regime's security system and place it on the defensive, immobilize its troops and make it fear attack on strategic nerve-centres without knowing how, when and from where attack would come. This was to be launched from all sides by numerous small armed groups operating separately, thus dispersing the regime's forces in pursuit of a fragmented organization and preventing it from concentrating its repressive apparatus against a compact target.

The disturbances caused by the urban guerrillas would be gradually increased, in order to immobilize governmental troops in the cities and prevent them from engaging the guerrillas in the interior. The emphasis would be on short, rapid attacks with maximum effectiveness, avoiding open clashes or decisive battles with the regime's forces, which would become a prey to alarm and growing nervous tension, expecting attack or following up a scent that would disappear. The urban guerrilla fighter should enjoy the maximum freedom of action and never renounce armed violence, helping to prepare the unleashing of the rural guerrilla

[1] The 'Mini-manual' was published as a supplement to 'Punto Final', April 1970, in Santiago, Chile.

[2] Ibid, p. 12.

13 Jollity back to back with austerity : Costa e Silva and Castello

14 President Costa e Silva

15 Professor Antônio Delfim Neto

16 Rio, June 1968 : having set fire to a police truck, rioting students go to work on a Volkswagen

17 Mounted police charge to disperse a crowd

18 President Emílio Garrastazu Médici

19 Football star Pelé

movement and to support it with the setting up of a revolutionary army of national liberation.

To fight his war, Marighela wanted men with a political motivation and technical training, to form a revolutionary nucleus, disciplined and indoctrinated with a long-term strategic and tactical view, consistent with the application of Marxist theory, of Leninism and 'Castro-Guevarism' to the conditions of Brazil. The urban guerrilla fighter, living in a society that he aimed to destroy, should be recruited from among a wide range of the Brazilian classes, from the workers, peasants, students, intellectuals, clergy and the womenfolk.

The Mini-Manual expressed its author's dedication and ruthlessness: 'for the urban guerrilla fighter, shooting and marksmanship are like air and water for the human being'. The 'revolution' needed money and expenses must be met by taking it from the capitalists, imperialists and land-owners, as well as from the government. The banking system was therefore a principal target and Marighela complained that the urban guerrilla met competition from the petty criminal ('marginal') in robbing, or as Marighela pompously said, 'expropriating' the banks. Defectors from his organization, however, accused him of maintaining a bank account in Switzerland under an assumed name.

From early 1968, the industrial areas of Brazil were also the scene of thefts of company wages, hijacking of airliners, bomb attacks on military installations, newspaper offices and American consulates, of the burning down of three television stations in São Paulo, as well as a host of assorted acts of violence, in which the guerrillas killed some 40 people and wounded about 180, including policemen, sentries, bank guards and various civilians.[1] The most publicized acts of terrorism were the kidnapping of foreign diplomats, including the American, West German and Swiss Ambassadors and a Japanese Consul-General, in exchange for whose release the terrorists compelled the government to release and transport abroad a large number of prisoners, most of whom had belonged to the various guerrilla groups.

Of these the Popular Revolutionary Vanguard, the National Liberation Alliance and the Revolutionary Movement of Octo-

[1] According to a press report covering the period from March 1967 to July 1970. It is estimated that in the rest of 1970 and up to August 1971, the guerrillas killed another 15 and wounded 70.

ber 8th (anniversary of 'Che' Guevara's last battle in Bolivia) were best known. At times, these groups would join forces for a particular action but generally they maintained a separate identity, much as Marighela had laid down. They often differed in their political ideology, but pursued the same objective, the overthrow of the regime in accordance with the strategy and tactics worked out by Marighela and the hard core of leaders, mostly veteran Communists. The body of these groups was mainly recruited from members of various Communist factions, from ex-soldiers 'purged' by the Movement of March 1964, and particularly from the students, among whom the leaders hoped to obtain recruits who would sever their links with society and become professional guerrilla fighters. The purges carried out by the Movement had hit the universities. Among the students, some of whom were attracted by the challenge of rebellion and of exciting, clandestine activity against a regime that they considered 'square' and oppressive, there appeared to be a continuing response to the call made by Marighela.

In 1971, after over three years of activity, only a provisional balance-sheet could be drawn up. By then, Marighela and his lieutenant, Joaquim Câmara Ferreira, as well as the third principal leader, ex-captain Carlos Lamarca, a crack marksman and counter-insurgency expert who deserted from the army, had died in ambushes or raids prepared by the security forces. The guerrillas had failed to damage industrial and business activity in the Centre-South. They had not multiplied in the cities in the manner that Marighela had planned; the prospect of escalation to a point where effective rural guerrilla activities could be launched against the regular army seemed remote. The leaders appeared to have overestimated the extent to which they would command popular support.

In the face of urban guerrilla activities, the mass of Brazilians, with a considerable capacity for non-involvement especially when bullets might be flying, did not appear to identify with the struggle of the urban guerrillas. Existing as small underground organizations, these were ill-placed to indoctrinate the masses and did not appear to have agreed on a programme for the future of Brazil. The seizure of foreign diplomats was anathema to a people naturally hospitable to foreigners and including large populations of foreign origin. Despite their considerable nuisance effects, the guerrilla actions had not built up to an urban rebellion and the army dealt with the outbreaks in the countryside where the guerrillas ultimately hoped to win over the peasants.

In Cuba, Castro had defeated a largely corrupt army and administration; it was surprising that Marighela should have believed that he could achieve the same result against a very different opposition in Brazil. The first phase of the guerrilla campaign appeared to end in failure, for lack of broad backing by the Left and inability to involve the industrial workers. It was problematical whether the guerrillas could overcome their internal problems and divisions and launch a second phase from a broader base of political support.

Although at great cost, the guerrillas obtained certain political dividends. Their activities helped to push the regime to the right, weakening the stand of the moderates and stimulating the move towards greater authoritarianism in government.[1] In the face of guerrilla action damaging to its prestige, the military regime introduced the death penalty for crimes against the national security and instituted banishment for those involved in terrorist activities. These had led the government to set up a large and sophisticated repressive apparatus to track down terrorists and cripple their organizations, involving police action over a broad front, where it interfered with the lives and privacy of the citizens, making the regime more unpopular.

There were also dividends to be obtained abroad. The tough, brutal methods used by the police in interrogating actual and suspected terrorists (after December 1968 without the inhibitions of habeas corpus), to secure information on the next kidnapping, bank robbery or bomb attack and to wring out information on the connections of those arrested, became known outside Brazil and damaged the regime's image abroad, where accusations of torture and brutality became common in the international press. In addition, the activities of the infamous 'death squads', which for a decade had with impunity been liquidating petty criminals, received wide publicity both in Brazil and abroad.

The second challenge: the student movement

The outbreak of intense political activity by students under the Costa e Silva regime was not surprising. Brazilian students have traditionally regarded themselves as an elite with the right and

[1] See Robert Moss, *Urban Guerrillas in Latin America* (Conflict Studies), London, October 1970.

even the duty to organize themselves and act politically.[1] For long, until a university education finally became a little more accessible, they were, in their meagre numbers and high social status, an upper-class elite that eventually broadened to include middle-class elements as new universities were formed. The course of events shows that they maintained a considerable level of political activity, as is common among Latin American students. Although a large proportion of Brazilian students has remained outside politics, the remainder has usually produced change-minded activists ready to agitate, tangle with the police and to 'sell' aggressively their own programmes to organize Brazil, invariably in ways unacceptable to the 'establishment' and requiring radical, revolutionary changes in Brazilian society.

Vargas periodically had trouble with them and was unsuccessful in trying to win their favour. From 1937 the students had their own union, the União Nacional de Estudantes (UNE), which provided a channel for them to try to influence the course of national politics; UNE however relied mostly on financial support from the government, although in later years it also obtained funds from the main political parties.

In the 1950s and '60s, UNE came under the dominance of various left-wing groups, despite a considerable effort made by the Church to maintain a youth organization—the Juventude Universitária Católica (JUC)—that would respond to leadership by the bishops. By the time of the Goulart regime, the leading elements running the UNE were Açâo Popular (Popular Action), JUC's independent, radical successor, and other groups broadly representing Soviet- and Chinese-line Communism, as well as Castroism.[2] UNE was among the various groups adopting a radical left-wing position and took part in all the political ferment of the closing period of the Goulart regime.

The Movement of March 1964 lost no time in dissolving the UNE, putting a damper on student political activities, and it was only at the end of 1966 and in 1967 that student activists came to life again. The great year for student protest and demonstra-

[1] Robert O. Myhr, 'The university student tradition in Brazil', *Journal of Inter-American Studies and World Affairs,* January 1970.

[2] Leonard D. Therry, 'Dominant power components in the Brazilian university student movement prior to April 1964', *Journal of Inter-American Studies,* January 1965.

tions was 1968, and it owed something to aggressive political activity by students in Europe—particularly in France during the summer of that year—and in the U.S.A. In Brazil, there was plenty to protest about—the backwardness of the universities, the military in power, the Americans in Vietnam and 'U.S. imperialism' in Brazil. Mass meetings, demonstrations in the streets, skirmishes with the police, who in São Paulo made cavalry charges, took place in most of the main cities; professional agitators joined in, bombs were planted, vehicles were burned and the police swung truncheons and broke heads.

In mid-year, following meetings of the National Security Council, the Minister of Justice issued an instruction to all federal, state and local authorities banning student demonstrations throughout Brazil. These were held from then on under the threat of severe police repression and various clashes between students and police occurred in Rio (where they were most serious), São Paulo, and other cities. In August the police invaded the Federal University of Brasília and at the end of September a conflict took place between Communist-influenced and anti-Communist groups of two São Paulo universities.

Meanwhile the administration sent to Congress various measures designed to reform the university system, but these gained little support from the students, who were uninterested in holding talks with the government. In October, there were further clashes between students and police, with the former demonstrating and striking in cities of the North, the North-East, and the Centre-South, two students being killed and various people being injured during repressive action by the state police in Rio.

The student movement suffered a serious setback when an attempt to hold a congress of the UNE in the country outside São Paulo was broken up by the police and army authorities, who arrested large numbers of students, including most of their leaders. Thereafter the average university campus was more quiet, but still a continuing source of opposition to the regime.

Ferment in the Church

The third challenge to the Costa e Silva regime came from the Church, which was now taking a much more direct interest in social and economic conditions.

The Church's increased involvement was largely in answer to

outside prompting and influence. From the 1930s a few of its leaders had responded to new ideas coming from Europe, but it was only in the 1960s that the Church reacted strongly to a new policy from Rome, expressed in the Second Vatican Ecumenical Council, the Encyclicals of Pope John XXIII, 'Mater et Magistra' and 'Pacem in Terris', and of Pope Paul VI, 'Populorum Progressio'. Pope John's discussion of the problems of under-development and of the question of colonialism found a ready echo in Latin America; Pope Paul's encyclical of March 1967 was interpreted as a charter for Christian social development and as giving Papal approval for structural reforms in Latin America. The issues at stake were debated during his visit to Colombia in 1968, when a Eucharistic Congress was held at Bogotá and a meeting of Latin American bishops took place at Medellín.

Established religion in Brazil was engaged in an uphill struggle. Long identified as a very conservative force in society, the Catholic Church faced internal problems: a 'crisis of vocations' resulting in a chronic shortage of priests, competition from Protestantism and the addiction of many of the poor to the cults brought to Brazil by the African slaves. It was a Church in decline, and had to find new strength and a new appeal.

The Church hierarchy included men who were ultra-conservative, conservative, moderate or 'progressive', with the last-named, led by Dom Helder Câmara, Archbishop of Recife, making up for lack of numbers by dynamism. Given this variety of attitudes, it was not surprising that it was difficult to reach a consensus upon how to conduct the process of the Church's renovation within the spirit of the Vatican Council and the Encyclicals.

Abruptly, the clergy were expected to change traditional attitudes. 'Suddenly injustice, poverty, backwardness, illiteracy, exploitation, became no longer trials imposed by God, which had to be borne humbly like rain and drought, disease and death, but man-made evils which, according to the Gospel, had to be combated. For the majority of the more or less faithful, the revolution of the Church remained incomprehensible; even a large portion of the clergy was caught completely off balance by it. For them, the revolution opened everything to question without providing clear-cut answers or replacing old guidelines with new, equally concrete ones.'[1] The shake-up in the Church

[1] Lorenz Stucki, 'Brazil's progressive priests', *Swiss Review of World Affairs,* April 1971, p. 19.

was in various respects beneficial. The new attitudes on social problems, for example, strengthened the hands of those priests who wished to take practical steps to improve the lot of the under-privileged, in other words, to assist the process of development.

In politics, relations between Church and State now became more confused and difficult to control. The Church's assembly, the National Conference of Bishops, emerged as a body able to speak independently on national problems and to make representations to the government, a role that was in many ways constructive. Beyond this sector, however, the potential area of conflict widened.

Some priests and lay brothers went their own way in digesting and applying the new ideas. Impatient to take action, they found themselves in sympathy with some of the ideas of Marxism. In economic matters, for instance, they turned against the 'injustice, greed and selfishness' of the capitalist system; for them, 'the Christian task was to destroy capitalism and fight against foreign imperialism'.[1] These men were a tiny minority in the Church but, inasmuch as they shared ideas held by others opposing the military regime, they gave rise to problems out of proportion to their numbers.

Thus, during the campaign by the Costa e Silva and Médici regimes to suppress the urban guerrilla movement, conflicts arose when members of the clergy were charged with being implicated in subversive activities; foreign-based religious orders were criticized, and some of their members arrested and tried for support of the guerrillas. The Church leaders found it necessary to protest against the methods used by the security forces. These events aggravated the crisis of 1968 when there was an increasing number of incidents involving the clergy and the authorities.

The Fifth Institutional Act

In this phase of increasing political difficulties and challenges, the regime lacked the necessary degree of leadership.

Among the military, for whom the strict maintenance of public order was indispensable, there was alarm at the disorders of 1968. There was growing criticism that the vigour and reforming mentality of the Movement had sharply declined. There was as yet little to show the public in terms of tangible improvements in their living standards and the widespread unpopularity of the

[1] Ibid, pp. 19-20.

military government added to the soldiers' feeling of frustration. Little was needed to bring their dissatisfaction to breaking-point.

In September 1968 the necessary incident occurred, when Márcio Moreira Alves, an opposition deputy, slighted the armed forces during a speech in Congress on the eve of Independence Day. The incident provided the means to bring matters to a head and gave to all among the military who were dissatisfied with the march of events an opportunity to insist that the President assert his authority.

The military demanded that Alves be deprived of his political rights. President Costa e Silva said that under the constitution this must be done by Congress, which in such cases was sovereign. Congress was not prepared to comply and, when the matter finally came up for decision, its vote against the measure included members of the governmental party, the Arena. Its refusal was rapidly followed by the issuing of the Fifth Institutional Act and the closure of Congress.

In the long, frustrating search for democratic, viable political institutions, representing the needs and aspirations of the people, the Fifth Institutional Act could be considered as one of the lowest points attained. It was watertight in its authoritarian content; it was the move to absolute power. Congress and the politicians were put into the 'deep freeze'. The Arena was alienated from the Executive, being criticized in the Justice Minister's speech introducing the Act. In its most ominous clause, 'habeas corpus' guarantees were suspended in the case of crimes against the national security or the economic and social order. Even wider powers were given for intervention in the states, and the Act reintroduced the suspension of political rights and the annulment of elective mandates. It shut off all the sources of political opposition and placed the press under direction.

The purge covered a broad field, including the Judiciary. Two judges of the Federal Supreme Court resigned and by presidential decree other judges hostile to the Movement were dismissed, the total number of judges being cut from 16 to 11. An investigating committee was set up under the chairmanship of a General to investigate, and recommend action against, those who had enriched themselves illicitly in the public service.

At regular intervals from January 1969 onwards, meetings of the National Security Council took place and lists were issued depriving politicians of their political rights. In due course, approximately 95 federal and about 150 state deputies and alternates were thus proscribed, the majority of them belonging to the opposition party, the MDB, but quite a substantial portion being members of the Arena.

Congress was in compulsory recess and military distrust of the politicians' conduct was further expressed by the closure, on charges of corrupt practices and irresponsibility, of the state legislative assemblies of São Paulo, Guanabara, Pernambuco, Rio de Janeiro, Sergipe, Pará and Goiás. The two political parties lost such prestige as they had enjoyed, but there seemed to be little public reaction of support for, or sympathy with, the party politicians.

The end of the Costa e Silva regime

The closing period of the Costa e Silva administration was taken up with two main lines of activity. The first was the continuation of the punitive political action under the terms of the Fifth Institutional Act: the federal government intervened in various municipalities in Paraná and Pernambuco.

The second was concerned with the ultimate resumption of political activities and the re-opening of Congress. The President directed the Vice-President, Pedro Aleixo, to work on drafting a revised version of the 1967 Constitution, and various persons, either cabinet ministers or jurists, were appointed to assist in this task. At the same time, decrees were issued announcing that municipal elections would be held in November, and arrangements were made for the holding of municipal, regional and national conventions of the Arena and MDB in order that a reorganization of the political parties be carried out and a fresh start be made. It was intended that when the President came to Rio at the end of August 1969, he should take the opportunity of promulgating the revised Constitution and ending the Congressional recess that had been decreed in the previous December. The President's health, however, was now failing. He began to feel indisposed in Brasília, but decided to go ahead with his plans and fly to Rio. The stroke that he then suffered immobilized him in the Laranjeiras Palace.

Economic recovery: the technocrats in power

In the Costa e Silva regime, political and economic affairs moved on different levels: as the former progressively deteriorated, the latter advanced firmly towards recovery.

Despite current difficulties when the new government took office, the economic situation had improved since April 1964. The Castello Branco administration had not by any means reached all its objectives but it had tackled a variety of tough problems, laying a foundation for its successor; the task of the new administration would be that much easier.

There were, however, many people in the cabinet or outside it anxious for new policies. Industry and business wanted action, particularly more credit, to lift them out of a serious recession. The Foreign Minister, Magalhães Pinto, stated that the policies of Roberto Campos and Professor Bulhões had failed, while the new Planning Minister, Hélio Beltrão, formerly director of a big department store, rejected their planning.

The Finance Minister, Professor Delfim Neto, said however that there would be no break in the continuity of the previous administration's policies. He followed its broad strategy but changed its tactics, enjoying in the process the support of President Costa e Silva. Delfim Neto was also a member of the new technocracy that now had a commanding voice in economic affairs. During the regime's two and a half years of office, he re-established the traditional position of the Finance Ministry as the centre of decision-making, and kept his own equilibrium on the tight-rope on which Brazilian Finance Ministers balance, at times precariously.

He took office at the age of 38, coming from the civil service and the university. Born in São Paulo of an Italian immigrant family of modest circumstances, he began his working life as a clerk in a state government office, studied economics in his spare time and graduated at São Paulo University, where he later joined the teaching staff. His university career was a stepping-stone: when Castello dismissed Adhemar de Barros from the São Paulo governorship in 1966, Delfim Neto joined the new state administration as Finance Secretary to restore order to its chaotic finances. The task was complex. Governor Adhemar, a colourful politician, who laid claim to the Virgin Mary's special protection and of whom Paulistas said 'he steals but he gets things done' ('rouba mas faz'), had made liberal use of the state funds for his own political purposes. From this post, with its key responsibilities, Delfim Neto's next move was to the federal Finance Ministry, a position that he held under Presidents Costa e Silva and Médici.

He was a self-made man, bred in a city that prides itself on offering possibilities of advancement to the hard-working; indeed, he frequently spoke of the need to create an open society that would enlarge the field of opportunities. Very much the technocrat—at his ease when lecturing with a blackboard to businessmen—he was also keenly interested in the political implications of policies. Almost a Mineiro in his political sense, he pursued for a time ambitions to the state governorship of São Paulo. Without the wide-ranging, international outlook of Roberto Campos, he believed in the merits of private enterprise, was strong on tactics and prepared to experiment, shunning drastic measures and acting cautiously in tackling inflation.

It was clear to him and to most that the Castello Branco regime's austerity policies would have to be relaxed. The early measures taken by the new administration were aimed to prevent any sharp rise in living costs and to grant relief to wage-earners, in line with the President's statements that something must be done to alleviate the lot of the poor and that his government would be guided by considerations of 'social humanism'. Few disagreed over the need to give the economy a 'shot in the arm'. Delfim Neto declared that the level of business and industrial activity must be raised; the economy had been at a standstill since the last quarter of 1966. Business and industrial interests in São Paulo expected action from the new Minister and did not want any more recessions. He said that it was imperative to bring about a resumption of economic activity through an increase in production and through steps to reduce costs in industry and business, although this must be done without causing a revival of inflation. In practice, the emphasis of government policy had now shifted to development, an eminently more popular objective.

The 'Strategic Development Programme'

The regime's economic blueprint, the 'Strategic Development Programme', was published in 1968 and covered the period from 1968-70; consisting of 15 volumes, it was prepared in six months by some 100 specialists from the public and private sectors, under the co-ordination of the Planning Minister, Hélio Beltrão.

Its introduction spoke of the challenge of Brazil, asked whether the country was viable, and affirmed that it was. Its diagnosis of the Brazilian problem, however, gave a long list of unfavourable symptoms. The economy was growing slowly but the population was increasing at an explosive rate: 850,000 new jobs a year had to be found for the new entrants into the labour market. There were considerable inequalities of income between individuals, sectors of the economy and regions of the country. There were also high rates of illiteracy and child mortality over extensive areas, serious deficiencies in transport, communications, health and housing. In education, public administration, agriculture and food supply, profound reforms were needed. There were vast empty spaces to be integrated with the rest of the country, large sectors of industry to modernize and mineral resources to be explored and identified. Tens of millions of Brazilians lived outside the market economy. It was not the first time that official spokesmen had declared that nearly everything in Brazil still remained to be done.

The Programme outlined three basic objectives of economic policy: the acceleration of economic development with the containing of inflation, the achievement of social progress and the expansion of employment opportunities.

Looking back on the sacrifices of the last three years, the authors of the Programme looked for a new strategy that would enable the country to resume and then surpass the high growth rates of the period before the decline in 1961. They took as a minimum target an annual growth rate of 6 per cent, but recognized that the country should be aiming for higher rates and that it was essential to involve the people as a whole, giving them confidence in the future and making them feel part of a national effort.

The Programme provided for increasing investment, laid down production goals for all the basic sectors of the economy and attended to regional development in the North-East and Amazônia. It declared that Brazil must expand its domestic market, aggressively build up its exports, develop its technical and scientific knowledge, and increase its domestic savings.

There was a suitable air of self-reliance in the language of the Programme. Development at the service of man must be accelerated and be the fruit of independent effort. The home market must be reserved for the expansion of industry already established in the country, a principal objective being to secure the well-being of the Brazilian entrepreneur, assisting him to compete in the future with the big foreign companies. The investment effort to achieve growth should not rely too much upon foreign capital to supplement domestic savings; the Brazilian economy itself was already capable of generating savings and reaching the necessary level of investment. The basic task of foreign resources would be to help maintain equilibrium in the balance of payments and to bring technology to Brazil.

It was an appropriate stance for a nationalist government, anxious to appear more forthrightly Brazilian than its predecessor.

Living with constant devaluations

'When a nation is stable, its money shows it. When the currency is debased, it is the whole nation that is degraded', said the *Jornal do Brasil,* Rio's leading daily, late in 1968.[1]

Not the least demoralizing fact of the Brazilian situation was the constant decline, at home and abroad, of the value of the cruzeiro, by any standards one of the world's shakier currencies. One of the innovations, during Prof. Delfim Neto's stewardship at the Finance Ministry, was the introduction of the 'crawling peg', a system of exchange-rate adjustments based on small frequent devaluations made at irregular intervals. Its Brazilian name, the 'flexible exchange-rate', could be criticized for over-optimism since, with the country's long experience of chronic inflation and currency depreciation, flexibility was in one direction only—downwards—and nobody could foresee when this trend would be reversed. An acceptance of the inevitable, the new system proved, however, to be realistic.

'We must put an end to this exchange rate Carnival', Delfim Neto was reported to have said, when the new system was introduced in August 1968. Certainly, the old method of large devaluations spaced out at long intervals gave the economy periodic 'hangovers', similar to those easily acquired at the Rio Carnival. With prices rising rapidly owing to inflation, speculation against the currency, in anticipation of the next devaluation, was a national pastime. To the canny speculator, religious festivals, bank holidays and Carnival were the obvious times for the authorities to devalue; individual citizens and powerful financial groups would all have dollar-buying sprees, with a fair assurance that they could not lose and with the prospect, if they guessed right, that they would make handsome profits when they cashed their dollars.

[1] Quoted in *Brazil in 1968,* Eric F. Lamb, Rio, January 1969, J. Henry Schroder Banking Corporation, p. 23.

Movements of capital to and from Brazil were subject to large, short-term swings. There was a natural and perfectly legal tendency for the big international companies operating in Brazil to remit heavily in the period before devaluation and to bring money in just after it, with alternating sharp reductions and increases of the country's exchange reserves. Exports were stimulated for a period after devaluation, but later lost their impetus and competitive power when the exchange rate was no longer realistic and favoured imports. There was a general pressure to increase prices as soon as devaluation took place. With exclamations of 'the dollar has gone up again' ('o dólar subiu') shopkeepers would justify to housewives substantial price increases that might be well above the rate of inflation.

The operation of the 'crawling peg' (with devaluations of between one and three per cent) pursued the goals of eliminating speculation, improving Brazil's export performance and ensuring a smoother flow of funds through the exchange system. In deciding the size and timing of devaluations, the authorities gave weight to the trend of domestic prices and costs, as well as to the foreign trade position and the level of the exchange reserves. The dates of payment of government obligations and the effects on living costs were also considered.

As to the results obtained, the new system neutralized speculation by drastically reducing the pickings; it brought more stability to the exchange sector and exchange crises no longer hit the headlines. In foreign trade, it contributed, together with other measures, to the process of building up Brazil's exports. It has been suggested that the dramatic improvement in the Brazilian trade position and the balance of payments dated directly from the introduction of the 'crawling peg', that no other factor could explain the 50 per cent increase in exports between 1968 and 1970.[1]

It was, in a number of ways, a success story, even if it was no real substitute for a determined policy to stabilize the value of the currency.

The Minister and the bankers

If Professor Delfim Neto seemed to have a favourite target for attack, then it was the nation's bankers, who were first called

[1] John Brooks, *Brazil: an economic survey, 1964-70,* London, Bolsa 1971, p. 9.

upon to co-operate voluntarily, but were later subjected to a regular yearly round of governmental regulation, the central point of which was the reduction of their interest rates. The cost of money was astronomical by European or American standards, 3 to 4 per cent a month being common in Brazil when inflation was at its height.

In the attempts to reduce it, the government imposed price controls on large sectors of industry, increased the efficiency of the tax collection and held down wages as far as it considered reasonable. To lower borrowing costs was about the only way left to help industry, and the banks and finance companies could without great harm be squeezed. Politically, moreover, this would be entirely in line with the call for greater austerity that found a ready appreciation among the armed forces. The campaign was accompanied by the necessary measures of psychological warfare on the bankers.

In April 1969 the Minister openly expressed his dissatisfaction with them by not attending their annual Congress in Curitiba. Later, in a press article he accused them of inefficiency and failure to appreciate the need for sacrifices in order to win the fight against inflation. While Hélio Beltrão castigated them as 'usurers of development', Delfim Neto charged them with speculation in high-class real estate on São Paulo's Avenida Paulista, where they were creating an 'under-developed Wall Street' at the expense of their customers in industry, commerce and agriculture. The banks would now be obliged to lower interest rates, the Minister said, and he let it be known that the government might acquire control of three commercial banks in order to ensure that effective action be taken.

This latter threat was unconvincing since through the powerful and highly profitable Bank of Brazil and, to a lesser degree, the big regional development banks such as the Bank of the North-East and the Bank of Amazônia, the government had ample instruments to make its weight felt throughout the whole financial system. In calling for austerity and a degree of sacrifice by the banks, however, the Minister was on firmer ground. The Prices Committee could hardly rigorously control prices charged by industrial and commercial firms, cutting off their credit at the Bank of Brazil if they overstepped the mark, unless they were compensated by lower interest rates.

Inasmuch as he sought to take forceful action against Brazil's chronic problem, inflation, Professor Delfim Neto had an enthusiastic press on this issue. Interest rates came down, but the measures taken did not have all the positive effects that the Minister would have liked to see. Inflation resisted his treatment and remained at the level of 24 per cent from 1967 through 1969.

The Fifth Institutional Act and the economy

The issuing in December 1968 of the Fifth Institutional Act was followed by a burst of activity on the economic front. The Congress having been abruptly ordered into recess, a spate of decrees was issued affecting the public and private sectors. No longer impeded by the 1967 Constitution, which it could amend at will, the administration was able to convert its decisions rapidly into law. From the view-point of Hélio Beltrão and Professor Delfim Neto, the Institutional Act was in many ways a godsend that gave them an opportunity to tackle afresh a number of serious problems.

In his official statements, Beltrão had been at pains to stress the positive benefits from the efforts made to step up development in 1968. The gross national product had achieved the highest growth rate in several years, he said. Exports had grown, employment had risen sharply and production of power, motor vehicles and ships had also increased substantially, following 18 months of improvement for much of business and industry. Advances had also been made in education, housing, transport and communications.

He did not mention, however, that during 1968 the fight against inflation had ground to a halt, with little hope of early improvement. The budget deficit remained uncomfortably high, all the non-inflationary means for its financing having been exhausted, and at the end of 1968 the administration was obliged to make the customary, large inflationary currency issues in order to pay its bills. The depreciation of the cruzeiro continued and the objective of its stabilization, frequently proclaimed, was about to disappear from sight.

With reinforced powers to deal with this situation, one of Delfim Neto's first moves was a constitutional amendment to reduce the deficit by boosting the government's share of the receipts from taxes on income and manufactured products, at the expense of the states and municipalities. By decree, ministries and governmental agencies were told to stop hiring staff and make a 10 per cent reduction in staff expenditure during 1969. With these measures and various budget cuts, he aimed to reduce the deficit by about two-thirds to a level at which it could be financed entirely with non-inflationary resources.

In the private sector, he ordered various measures to develop the capital market, one of the weakest links in the financial system, and to strengthen the financial situation of private firms and companies. In other sectors, an attempt was made to return to greater austerity. The setting up of a commission to investigate illicit enrichment by those in the public service, the doubling of import duties on luxury goods, the tougher line taken against contraband and the attempt to crack down on the usual round of automatic price increases by tradespeople at the beginning of the year, were symptomatic of the abandonment in the economic sector of President Costa e Silva's well-intentioned, permissive policy of 'humanization'.

As Brazil slumped to a low political level late in 1969, the economic boom was beginning. Agriculture was responding to various stimuli, and industrial production went up by over 15 per cent in 1968 and over 10 per cent in 1969. In these two years the overall economic growth rates were 8½ and 9 per cent respectively. The technocrats had found the answers to some of Brazil's problems.

7 The Médici Government

The interregnum

At the end of August 1969, President Costa e Silva lay disabled in the Laranjeiras Palace in Rio. The responsibilities of government were at once assumed by the three service ministers, General Lyra Tavares, Admiral Augusto Rademacker and Air Marshal Souza e Mello, the military leaders having rapidly decided that the constitutional successor, the civilian Vice-President, Pedro Aleixo, should not take office. Banks and stock exchanges closed for a day, and, having little choice, the country reacted calmly to the crisis.

The period of the interregnum was one of tension. Early in September a guerrilla group in Rio seized Mr. Charles Burke Elbrick, the American Ambassador, in circumstances that provided a severe test for the triumvirate of ministers and a humiliating experience for the government, which was obliged to yield to the group's demand for the release of prisoners, in exchange for the freedom of the Ambassador. Political attitudes immediately hardened: decrees were issued introducing the penalties of banishment or death for crimes of subversion and revolutionary war.

These events emphasized the urgency for Brazil to establish a government of authority; the caretaker government of the military ministers could only be a stop-gap measure, pending decision in the armed forces as to the future of the Presidency. Following a visit by a French specialist who confirmed Costa e Silva's inability to return to the Presidency—he died in December—intensive meetings took place amongst the military on the problem of succession. There was 'intense political campaigning among officers, even polling of officer opinion down to the battalion level, and the issuance of numerous manifestos'.[1] After a long process of argument and negotiation, during which the nationalist officers, whose candidate was General Albuquerque Lima, made an unsuccessful bid for power, the views of the senior officers prevailed in nominating General Emílio Garrastazu

[1] Alfred Stepan, *The Military in Politics,* p. 264.

Médici, a 64-year-old four-star general, who was commander of the Third Army in Pôrto Alegre and had previously served under Costa e Silva as head of the national information service. The Presidency and Vice-Presidency were declared vacant and preparations were made for General Médici and Admiral Rademacker to take office at the end of October.

Meanwhile, the military ministers, to the surprise of those who had forecast the shelving of Costa e Silva's policy of political relaxation, went ahead with the various measures that he had intended to implement: Congress was recalled, ending the ten-month recess begun in December 1968, and a revised version of the 1967 Constitution was promulgated. Nevertheless, powerful safeguards were retained. The Fifth Institutional Act remained in force and a further decree gave the new President powers to deal with officers whose actions prejudiced the unity of the armed forces, thus protecting him from the activities of military pressure groups.

The new administration

The administration of President Médici, which began in October 1969 and was scheduled to serve until March 1974, took as its starting-point the restoration of military unity.

The composition of his cabinet showed his intention of governing with broadly-based support from the armed forces, whose unity had been seriously weakened under the Costa e Silva regime and severely tested in the period of caretaker government. President Médici brought into the government officers who had been closely associated with the late President Castello Branco, whose influence had for some time been in eclipse. At the same time, he ensured continuity in policies by retaining various members of Costa e Silva's cabinet, including Professor Delfim Neto and Colonel Mário Andreazza, the Transport Minister. He insisted that his ministers abandon political ambitions and concentrate on their jobs; he gave evidence of intending to control them with a tighter rein than his predecessor and to give a more direct lead in decision-making.

Unlike Castello, who was at home in politics and had many friends outside the army, or Costa e Silva, who from his youth had taken part in public life, Médici was exclusively a military man. He assumed the Presidency reluctantly, with commitments only to the armed forces, and as a further duty to be done.

Deliberate and methodical, he had a staff officer's belief in thorough briefing and, as former head of the national information service, had already acquired a grounding in the national problems.

President Médici sought to renew the basic ideas of the Movement of March 1964, restating them in a disquisition on 'the great national task' contained in one of the regime's policy documents.[1] This saw the 'revolution' of 1964 as a completion of the cycle of 'revolutions' that the Republic had suffered in the past. Those of 1930 and 1945 had understood the need for political reforms to eliminate the old oligarchies and had been aware of social injustices, but had not been fully conscious of the primary importance of development.

The 'revolution' of 1964, in its authenticity, was destined 'to create basic conditions for genuine development, democracy and sovereignty', the document declared. Development must be directed to the benefit of all, with full participation of the middle and working classes in its fruits. Genuine democracy implied the supersession of the oligarchies in the states and municipalities, the renewal of values and the reform of institutions; sovereignty required that the country make the effort of organizing itself and of working and acting efficiently in the creation of its own development. The achievement of this required a government without commitments to the interests of groups, classes, sectors or regions, and able to make the structural changes that would ensure Brazil's viability as a great power.

The document recognized the extent of hard preparation needed if Brazil was to take its place among the countries of the developed world which, it hoped, would become a more open one. It looked at this preparation, in the first instance, in economic terms. The country must advance along the road to more rapid self-sustaining development, to a relative stability of prices in a climate of security and of social and political stability. In the last respect, a realistic effort would be made to evolve towards the building of a politically open society that would reconcile the need for faster development with the maintenance of the freedoms, with the greatest possible degree of participation by private enterprise and the decentralization of economic activity.

It was a doctrine of the technocracy. Spokesmen for the regime

[1] The *'Goals and bases of Government action'*, published in Rio in September 1970.

would say that, through an economically open society, they wanted to move to one that was politically open. The question was how an advance could be made, in view of the realities of the regime's commitments to its base of support in the armed forces.

At home, the Médici government faced the threats and irritations caused by the urban guerrillas, while the degree of power and independence of a frequently vicious security organization scarcely helped the regime's image. Nevertheless, as time went by, the government appeared to grow in self-confidence. In foreign affairs it continued the process of detaching Brazil from the dominant influence of the U.S.A.; it extended the territorial waters of Brazil to a 200-mile limit and began to build up its strength as a maritime and naval power. Brazilian diplomacy became more active in approaching its neighbour countries with proposals for co-operation in regional development schemes.

In the early days of his administration, President Médici expressed intentions to foster a closer relationship with Congress and the politicians, saying that the opposition would have a role to play. The problem remained, however, of what constructive relationships could be established between an all-powerful Executive and a Legislature composed of the tattered remnants of the old political classes. The Costa e Silva regime, particularly through the actions of its Minister of Justice, Gama e Silva, had left little scope for positive measures, as far as political life was concerned.

Médici began with the hope of planting something in this barren soil. His initial public statements, with their admission that the regime was undemocratic, their conviction that there were solutions to Brazil's recurrent political crises and the hope that, at the end of his mandate, democracy would be established, were shown by experience of office to be over-optimistic. By the end of February 1970, when he said that the Fifth Institutional Act had come too late and when he admonished what was left of the nation's politicians, President Médici appeared to be akin to the 'hard liner', although, as time went on, he emerged as a moderate. In his relations with the official party, the Arena, he seemed to issue orders rather than exercise constructive political leadership, but there was perhaps little alternative under the circumstances. This was shown to be the case when he selected Arena candidates for the elections for state governors to be held later in the year.

The criterion used for picking the new governors was their acceptability to the Movement of March 1964. The choices fell on administrators and frequently on engineers, men unconnected with the old political classes. In the key state of São Paulo, President Médici played safe in choosing Laudo Natel, who could be relied upon to work smoothly with the regime. As far as the opposition stronghold of Rio was concerned, he acquiesced in the MDB's choice of Chagas Freitas, a newspaper owner; only in the case of the state of Bahia did the President make a choice that was popular with the local politicians, in nominating Antônio Carlos Magalhães, the Mayor of Salvador.

The supremacy of football

Did party politics really matter to Brazilians? Not apparently in 1970, when the nation was gripped by the fever of the World Cup football finals taking place in Mexico.

In Brazilian cities, there is already a Carnival atmosphere with fireworks, banners and pageantry at the local football 'derbies', when Flamengo plays Fluminense in Rio or Corintians meets São Paulo, when Cruzeiro play Atlético in Belo Horizonte or Internacional plays Grêmio in Pôrto Alegre. This is nothing in comparison with what happens when Brazil is playing in the World Cup. Then there is a religious fervour, otherwise a rare occurrence; whole cities erupt in fireworks and petards when Brazil scores a goal, even São Paulo, whose citizens are not given to displays of emotion and excitement. Thus, the exploits of the star players, Pelé, Tostão, Jairzinho, Rivelino and company, commanded in Mexico by a brigadier, were what mattered to the nation in 1970. Victory in the World Cup for the third time, with the permanent holding of the Jules Rimet trophy, was a national vindication and a boost to the Brazilian ego, of political, economic and social importance in its stimulus to the national self-confidence.

It was also a boost for the government. Coming from the town of Bagé near the Uruguayan border, President Médici was a cavalry officer and a 'gaúcho de chimarrão'[1] a man of middle-class family virtues and genuinely a football fan. He was as averse to self-advertisement as Castello, but his advisers, conscious of the remoteness of the regime from the people, took the opportunity to enhance, and reap political benefit from, the national

[1] Chimarrão: the bitter maté (Paraguayan tea) drunk from a tube and bowl by the gaúchos in the cattle country of South Brazil.

mood of elation. After the football triumph, they brought out the slogans and the sticker labels, from the President's 'No one can stop this country' ('ninguém segura este país') to 'Brazil, love it or leave it!', 'Brazil, I'm staying!' and 'Brazil, count on me!' Rio's satirical weekly *O Pasquim* ('Lampoon'), required reading for Cariocas on the beaches or in the cafés, was not prepared to take things that seriously and looked at them with characteristic irreverence; taking Médici's slogan, it portrayed a peasant on an icy slope, struggling desperately to stop a heavily-loaded sledge from careering down the mountainside.

In the political sense, the country was hardly on the path towards developing democratic political institutions, but economically speaking it looked as though the slogans were right.

The economics of confidence

The policies worked out by the technocrats were now plainly bearing fruit. The gross domestic product had risen by 9.5 per cent in 1970 and the level of investment was increasing. The federal budget looked strong; the balance of payments had shown large surpluses in 1969 and 1970 and Brazil's gold and foreign exchange reserves had soared to unprecedented heights. So had the foreign debt, under the impact of the foreign loans that had been contracted, but there was official confidence in the country's capacity to discharge its obligations in view of the remarkable expansion of exports, which had nearly doubled from 1964 to 1970. Many sectors of industry were expanding and important new ventures in petrochemicals were being launched. Inflation was hardly being reduced but it was under control, or at any rate tamed; interest in reducing it substantially had somewhat waned amidst the enthusiasm over the high growth rates.

The Médici administration added to the abundant literature of development programmes prepared since 1964, in its 'Goals and bases for Government action' published in 1970, and in its Development Plan for 1972-4 issued a year later. The targets were becoming more ambitious. The Plan's chief objectives were to place Brazil among the developed countries of the world within a generation; to double income per head between 1969 and 1980, raising it to 500 dollars by 1974; to increase the gross domestic product by 8-10 per cent a year up to 1974, to reduce the annual rate of inflation to about 10 per cent and to increase the level of employment.

The national priorities were set: a 'revolution' in education and an acceleration of health and hygiene programmes, a 'revolution' in agriculture and food supply, the speeding up of scientific and technological development and the strengthening of the competitive power of national industry.

The specific targets included: between 1972 and 1974 increases of at least 10 and 8 per cent in the values of exports and imports; a large rise in exports of manufactures during the same period; and maintenance of international reserves at a level of about 1,400m. dollars; the installation of 1m. new telephones by 1974 and the reduction of the number of illiterates between the ages of 15 and 35 from 7m. to 2m.

The administration recognized that since 1964 an expansion had taken place in education but that as yet there had been little of the required 'revolution'. Under Médici, the Movement of March 1964 seemed to react to the need to tackle the nation's number one problem more aggressively. Costa e Silva had appointed as Education Minister a run-of-the-mill politician who impressed no one, but in the new administration the post went to Jarbas Passarinho, a man of political acumen and more able to communicate with youth. A better directed effort now began to improve the quality and productivity of education, as well as to integrate it with scientific and technological development.

A further overdue step was the setting up within the Ministry of the Brazilian Movement for Literacy (Mobral) which was headed by Mário Henrique Simonsen, a leading economist and adviser to governments since 1964. Mobral's targets were to teach 4.5m adults to read and write by the end of 1973; it worked through state and municipal departments of education, and private firms were given the opportunity of supporting Mobral by handing over to it from 1 to 2 per cent of their income tax liabilities. 'You too are responsible' was the slogan that appeared on posters throughout the country, in an effort to awaken public opinion to the magnitude of the illiteracy problem.

Social integration

'We reach the unsavoury conclusion that the economy may prosper but most of the people live badly', President Médici said in a speech in Recife.

To the foreign visitor, it is often a mystery how the poor manage to live in Brazil, how manual labourers, many of whom receive the minimum wage (currently the equivalent of about £17 a month) can exist, let alone raise families. In the less-developed regions, such as the North-East, the worker may in fact receive less than the minimum and in all respects live badly. Even in the cities and towns of the more developed Centre-South, the living conditions of the poor are often marked by inadequate housing and the lack of the basic sanitary facilities. Unskilled labour is in surplus; unemployment and under-employment exert pressure on wage-rates.

In a country as unevenly developed as Brazil, the problems of reducing the areas of poverty and improving the living standards of the people do not lend themselves to rapid solutions. The situation requires a massive, sustained development effort over many years: the national income, the 'cake', must be increased in order to make larger 'slices' for all. Equally, however, when this is happening, the question is posed of how to ensure that the fruits of development are not simply absorbed by the 'haves' but actually reach the 'have-nots'.

President Vargas had tried to tackle these problems by welfare legislation and protection of the workers' earnings. The Movement of March 1964 had created an effective taxation system and the Médici administration looked for further ways of distributing the benefits of development, by attempting to integrate the worker into the economic system. In introducing its proposals, the government spoke in broad terms of wishing to create a more open and developed society, but the actual scheme probably also represented military wishes to try to identify their new order of things more closely with the people.

The 'social integration' programme, announced in August 1970, stemmed from these attitudes. It appears that President Médici had wanted to go further than in practice he did: workers' participation in company profits and management was mooted, but this was dropped in the face of opposition from businessmen and industrialists who argued that such schemes had not worked in any other country. In the event, the programme involved contributions by government and employers. In establishing a participation fund, the government waived its right to receive a proportion (initially 2 per cent) of firms' income-tax liabilities; this would be handed over to the fund and the firms themselves would pay in a fraction (up to one half per cent) of their turnover.

Each employee would receive an initial capital that would be entered in a savings book and would grow with the yearly addition of interest, monetary correction and profits from the administration of the fund by the Federal Savings Bank, providing him with a 'nest-egg' available for making a down payment on a house, for getting married, for retirement or disablement. He could, however, draw out the money from interest and monetary correction annually if he wished. A low-paid worker would, it was claimed, receive up to two monthly minimum wages annually from the fund in the form of interest and monetary correction, and on retirement, after 30 years, would be paid about two years' wages. The fund, which, it was suggested, might reach the equivalent of about £500 m. by 1974, was to have other purposes. The Savings Bank would build it up by investments in the stock-market and in other forms of financing; the fund would also provide working capital to private enterprise, and the government gave an assurance that it would not use it to finance its own undertakings.

President Médici hoped that the programme would lead to harmony between capital and labour; it was Brazilian in its ingenuity and one hoped that it would be efficiently administered.

A new capitalism?

From 1964 the new technocracy, with military backing, was intent on modernizing Brazilian capitalism.

Industry and business had grown up behind high protective tariff barriers and in the hothouse atmosphere of chronic inflation. They were not, the technocrats argued, organized to serve the mass home-market that it was hoped ultimately to bring into being; nor would they be able to compete with foreign companies in the international markets that Brazil must in due course attempt to enter.

Capitalism was of the old school and the 'management revolution' long established in the U.S.A. and Western Europe, had made little headway in Brazil. Of the country's 244,500 firms, less than 5 per cent were constituted as corporations and of these only 400 had opened their capital to public subscription.[1] The overwhelming majority of the firms were individual businesses or ones owned by families or closed financial groups. In 1970,

[1] American Chamber of Commerce, *Brazilian News Briefs,* June 1971.

however, 50 per cent of the firms' income tax payments to the government were contributed by the corporations.

In the post-1964 dispensation, it was decided that firms should be persuaded to 'democratize' their capital, opening it to the public, and a range of tax exemptions and deductions was granted to those undertaking to do so. The technocrats' idea was that a company prepared to offer voting rights to public shareholders would be more likely to manage its business and keep its books in a manner conforming to modern standards. At the same time, firms that under conditions of chronic inflation had financed themselves by short-term loans from the banks would become accustomed to raising capital in the stock-market, in accordance with the methods used in the more developed countries, thus increasing the volume of funds available for investments.

The objective was to foster a modern capitalism able to cater to a mass-market, in contrast to existing business and industry, as the technocrats saw them, with their practices of charging high prices on a low output. Businessmen, who in the past had suffered from, and adapted themselves to, bureaucracy and corruption in government, were now subject to a certain degree of tutelage. From 1967 particularly, when Professor Delfim Neto said that efforts must be directed to reducing the inflation of costs, businessmen were expected to work closely with the economists and civil servants running the agencies concerned with price control.

The technocrats had limited success in persuading the capitalists to 'democratize' capital, but they made stronger efforts to create a shareholding mentality. The Capital Market law of 1965 had been a first step in the development of an authentic stock-market and early in 1967 a scheme was introduced allowing taxpayers to use part of their income-tax liabilities in the purchase of shares in private companies.[1] This was a further attempt to strengthen corporate finance but it was also a move to encourage a 'capitalism of the greater number', ultimately a 'popular capitalism' that would give more people a stake in the 'system'. The regime's intentions in this respect were further expressed in the social integration programme discussed above.

Brazilians are quick-witted in financial matters, born speculators. Once they had become convinced that the government was

[1] This was the Decree-Law 157 scheme.

fully behind the development of the stock-market and was competent to sustain it, investors large and small joined in. To foreigners used to sophisticated markets and venerable stock exchanges, it required some mental adjustment to fathom the type of pump-priming, forced-growth operation undertaken in the capital market in Brazil. But for Brazilians it seemed to have a fascination and they were ready to put their money into it; in 1970 and 1971 there were very large increases in the volume of transactions on the Rio and São Paulo stock exchanges.

Was there a role for foreign capital in the new order of things after 1964?

Foreign capital had been established in Brazil for some time, particularly in the shape of the international companies strongly represented in São Paulo, where Volkswagen had 'put Brazil on wheels'. In such industries as motor vehicles, pharmaceuticals and telecommunications equipment the foreign presence looked large, especially to exponents of the extreme forms of Brazilian nationalism. In the overall national picture, official figures might suggest that foreign capital was not all that dominant, accounting for around 3.5 per cent of the total capital stock of the country, at the end of 1969.[1] In their daily life, however, Brazilians constantly found themselves using products made, admittedly in Brazil, by foreign companies.

The post-1964 regimes were anxious to consolidate and increase the competitive power of native-born industry and business, and took steps to strengthen them; the technocrats looked for more effective performance by Brazilian private enterprise and encouraged the formation of large companies able to compete abroad.

It seemed that, in view of the huge tasks of development and the shortage of capital, there would be room for a degree of new foreign participation, within certain limits. For example, the foreigner had a contribution to make in the introduction of 'know-how' and technology and he was also a source of loan finance. Brazilians might wish to have the advantages of foreign capital without having to suffer the foreign capitalist, but the evidence indicated that the government was prepared to be pragmatic in considering what was in the national interest.

The Médici administration looked for 'a consolidation of an

[1] Central Bank figures quoted in 'Brazil: an economic survey', by the First National City Bank, New York, 1971, p. 14.

economic system of balance between the government and the private sector, with the presence of the public enterprise, of national and of foreign private enterprise in proportions ensuring that the system will remain economically and politically viable'.[1] At a time when other South American countries, such as Chile, were shutting out traditional foreign interests, Brazilian nationalism was prepared to be more flexible and less dogmatic than its neighbours in Spanish America.

Regional programmes

The weather played its part in helping to focus the Médici administration's attention on the problems of the other Brazil, of the North-East and Amazônia.

President Médici visited the North-East at the height of the drought in 1970 and one would expect its parched landscape to have made an impression on a man accustomed to the rich, green countryside of southern Brazil. After the visit, the administration brought out a national integration programme.

In a reaction to the drought, the programme included implementation of the first stage of a national irrigation scheme and settlement of the humid valleys of the North-East. It contained, as a principal instrument, the construction of a Transamazonian highway, with the launching of colonization programmes along its course. This road, crossing Central Amazônia from east to west, a distance of over 1,500 miles, was to combine with existing highways and run from the Atlantic to the Peruvian border; together with a 940-mile north-south road to be built from Santarém in Amazônia to Cuiabá in the Centre-West, it was intended to fulfil a role of national integration, creating a system of communication between the Centre-West, Amazônia and the North-East.

In high-flown language, the regime claimed that Brazil was pushing its economic frontiers up to the banks of the Amazon; that a strategy of economic occupation of Amazônia was being integrated with a development strategy for the North-East. Officials hoped that new agricultural areas would be opened up, that the new roads would assist the discovery and exploitation of minerals, and that the surplus population of the North-East would find its way to this 'new frontier' rather than to the already congested cities of the Centre-South. Settlers in the new

[1] 'Goals and bases of Government action', Rio, 1970, p. 10.

areas were, however, likely to face daunting obstacles, particularly health problems, in their life as pioneers.

The Médici regime's second programme, published in 1971, was the agrarian 'Proterra', aimed at improving the lot of the rural populations in the North and the North-East. Its purpose was to put substantial funds into acquiring land for small and medium-sized farms, financing the expansion of farming and helping to organize and modernize rural properties. Money was also to be used in financing the establishment of agrarian industries, including the production of sugar, seeds and fertilizers, and in improving research programmes and storage and distribution facilities.

Through the Proterra, the regime hoped to offset the pronounced bias in the two regions towards the development of industry and hence to the growth of the cities. The ultimate aim was to create genuine farming communities from the thousands of subsistence farmers working with primitive methods and unable to contribute effectively with produce for the market or themselves to offer a market for the products of industry.

President Médici summed up the intentions of government in its aspirations to transform the economic and social face of the North and the North-East, to promote the integration of Amazônia into the national community and to wrest the North-eastern populations from their penury. There were interests in both regions anxious to maintain the *status quo* and hostile to change; it remained to be seen if yet another programme would get to grips with long-standing problems.

8 The Other Brazil: The North-East

> Brazil is an empire, within whose confines are to be found areas that are metropolitan in their development and areas in a state of colonial dependency.
>
> José Honório Rodrigues, *The Brazilians, their Character and Aspirations*

'Within our national frontiers, we have not only a Belgium but also a Kenya, a Nigeria and a Pakistan—a diversity that is part of our country's greatness but is also its misfortune', Professor Vamireh Chacon told the author in Recife, capital of the state of Pernambuco and the North-East's largest city. 'It is our bad luck in this region that we are suppliers of cheap labour to the remainder of the country', he added. His comments, illustrating the glaring contrasts of development in Brazil, also indicated how conscious North-easterners are of their unfavourable situation in comparison with their fellow-countrymen in the Centre-South.

The visitor to the North-East soon grasps that he is in another Brazil, in what is in many respects a 'country within a country'. He senses the change of atmosphere when he arrives in Recife from Rio or São Paulo, or indeed from Salvador, state capital of Bahia, another of the North-East's big cities, which up to 1763 was the capital of Brazil and today retains a pride in its past. In Salvador, although there is some poverty, there is a friendliness and optimism typical of an attractive, colourful city where the Brazilian negro and his folklore have had a positive influence on the local culture.

The thin, taciturn Pernambucanos think differently, however. In Recife there is little optimism in the faces of the people or in the aspect of the city, even when a progressive administration runs the beggars out of town and undertakes extensive public works to improve the city's appearance and amenities. Pernambuco is the most highly politicized of the North-eastern states and in it the region's position stands out more sharply. The

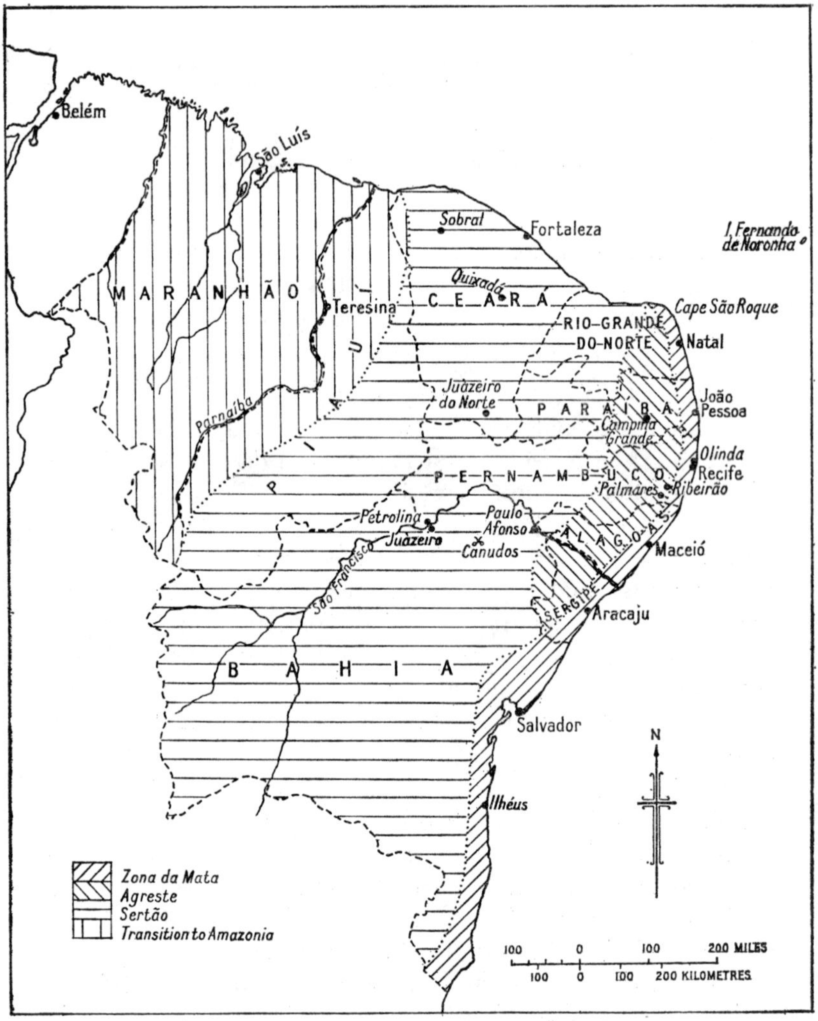

2 North-eastern Brazil

visitor detects feelings of disillusionment. Some of the local people recall that the North-East was once the national centre of things, and they consider that through its trading activities it made a major contribution by providing funds for the development of what is now the Centre-South. They regret that the North-East has for some time been relegated to the status of a problem-region needing the support and the money of the Centre-South, which exercises an undisputed national leadership that they have often resented. The visiting businessman and industrialist from São Paulo, which for decades has absorbed refugees from the North-East, is not therefore always regarded with much sympathy.

Recognized as a key element of the Brazilian problem, the North-East offers the toughest challenge to the efforts to integrate, develop and modernize the country. If Vamireh Chacon, a university professor, trained in sociology in Western Germany and in economics by Chicago University, spoke of its position within the country in balanced terms, others have been very outspoken on North-eastern problems, particularly on the living-conditions of the people. Dom Helder Câmara, since 1964 Archbishop of Recife and Olinda, the most politically active member of the Church hierarchy and an exponent of 'Third World' ideas, wrote, with particular reference to his own archdiocese: 'The abolition of slavery must be completed. After we freed ourselves from that disgrace of the Americas—the enslavement of Africans—the slavery of our own peoples took root in our continent. May 13th 1888[1] must be brought to its conclusion'.[2]

Dom Helder, a small, frail-looking Cearense from Fortaleza, who was a friend of Pope Paul VI and led the Church's 'progressive' wing in Brazil, did not mince his words—and he spoke a great deal—when addressing himself to national or even international problems. An idol of the North-eastern poor and popular among Brazilian youth, he was frequently the centre of controversy. He was not exactly in his element when he attempted to promote the reform of the capitalist and international economic systems; but he was much more convincing in his reformist activities in the North-East, where the Church had a significant contribution to make, and where his readiness to 'stir things up' and to protest against what he considered were

[1] The date of the abolition of slavery in Brazil.

[2] *Revolução dentro da paz,* Editôra Sabiá, Rio, p. 145.

the abuses and failings of government, made him very unpopular with the authorities.

The North-eastern geography

A large territory of almost 600,000 sq. miles, which accounts for 18 per cent of the land area of Brazil and, with over 28m. people, for some 30 per cent of its population, the North-East lies on, and to the north-west and south-west of the pronounced bulge of the Atlantic coast-line where Brazil is closest to Europe and Africa. There are nine states in the North-East and some are giants.[1] The southernmost of them, Bahia, is larger than France; states like Maranhão and Piauí, unknown to Europeans, are larger than Italy and Great Britain respectively, while the whole Common Market area of the 'Six' would fit easily into the North-East, with room to spare. It is larger in area than any country in South America, except Argentina. The size of the territory is, however, matched by its backwardness, and it is the most extensive individual under-developed area in the American continent.

Possessing a climate typical of equatorial and tropical regions, the North-east presents quite wide variations in rainfall, vegetation and fertility, and may conveniently be broken down into four sub-regions. From the south of Bahia to that part of Rio Grande do Norte where the coast turns sharply west, runs a green, humid and fertile coastal belt some 50 miles deep, containing most of the principal cities and fully a quarter of the North-East's population. This is the 'Zona da Mata', literally 'woodland' or 'forest zone', so named by the Portuguese settlers who cut down the thick tropical forests and planted sugar-cane. Behind part of it, from Sergipe to Rio Grande, lies a broader, semi-humid zone, the 'Agreste' (meaning wild or rustic), source of most of the region's basic foodstuffs and an area of transition to the interior; between them, these two sub-regions cover 10 per cent of the area of the North-East and contain 39 per cent of its population. The coast continues north-westward past Ceará and Piauí to Maranhão, where the typically North-eastern features of the land gradually alter and we enter a territory, much larger than the first two sub-regions but thinly populated, of transition to Amazônia.

[1] The states are: Alagoas, Bahia, Ceará, Maranhão, Paraíba, Pernambuco, Piauí, Rio Grande do Norte and Sergipe.

Finally, occupying more than half of the North-East is the great mass of the interior, the semi-arid 'Sertão', or backlands, usually also taken to include most of Rio Grande do Norte and all Ceará. Here lives rather less than half of the North-eastern population. It is an area of irregular and unequally distributed rainfall and from its odd, unstable conditions came the sertão's characteristic vegetation, the 'caatinga', which with the scrub and grass-lands, composes the general landscape. Spiny shrubs, stunted trees and cactus, able to live on for months and even years without rain, make up the grey wilderness of the caatinga, which is dense in the wetter areas and, when the rain comes, undergoes a lightning, green transformation.

Within the expanse of the sertão, there is cattle-raising, carried on by the landowners over extensive areas,[1] cotton growing and primitive subsistence agriculture; their labour force, the people of the sertão or 'sertanejos', working as ranch-hands and share-croppers, or at times moving off in large numbers to the coastal areas to work for a season on the cane-harvest. Independent and ascetic, accustomed to a dry climate and broad horizons that give them a sense of freedom, the sertanejos contrast with the people of the coastal areas, where they seldom feel at home. More than one authority writes of their attachment to the harsh land in which they live and of their eagerness to return to it.

Landowners, bandits and mystics

These broad spaces of the North-eastern interior, with their poverty, lack of communications and minimum of governmental control, were long the stronghold of a feudal society, dominated by the big landowning families of the 'colonels' (an honorary rank in the state militia) whose word was law and who employed their own gunmen, the 'cabras' or 'capangas', to deal with their enemies, protect their property or to extend it by seizure. At its best, this society was paternalistic, with the landowner attending to the welfare of the peasant in return for his allegiance. At its worst, it was arbitrary and unjust, creating among the people conditions for the two extremes of reaction against oppressive social conditions: that of the outlaw and of the mystic. The expanse of the sertão offered favourable conditions for the proliferation of banditry, which found there freedom of manoeuvre and a refuge from pursuit by the forces of law and

[1] See G. Phelps, *The Last Horizon,* pp. 105-10.

order, such as they were. A long line of bandits and outlaws, the 'cangaceiros', from time to time dominated large areas of the sertão, defying the authorities, attacking the farms and estates, pillaging and at times joining in local politics. The most famous of them, 'Lampeão', saw himself as a scourge of the wealthy and protector of the poor, and had his own ideas as to how local government should be carried on. He led a well-armed and quite disciplined force but was finally eliminated by federal troops in 1938 after a bloody battle.

No less numerous in the environment of the sertão were the religious visionaries, miracle-workers, penitents and cranks, and among this company two men especially left their mark upon the mentality and folklore of the people.

Antônio Maciel, the 'Counsellor', came from a locality in Ceará rent by a violent family feud complete with massacres and acts of revenge. For years he roamed the sertão as a vagrant. Gaining popular recognition as an ascetic, towards the end of the nineteenth century he set up at Canudos in the Bahian interior a community to which flocked people from all over the North-East, attributing to him supernatural powers and blindly following his leadership. Absolute ruler of his 'New Jerusalem' where he enforced discipline, upheld family life and respected the organization and rites of the church, he became the exponent of a backlands religion that was 'a crude mixture of Catholic rites, African witchcraft and Indian Superstition'.[1] The Counsellor's 'stolid devotees knew nothing about the world at large and cared less. About Brazil, they understood vaguely that it was a republic of masons who had expelled the old Emperor and instituted civil marriage, acts that struck them as displaying unpardonable irreverence'.

The Counsellor eventually fell foul of the local authorities and the Republican government, which he vilified; they accordingly decided that he should be eliminated. It did not prove an easy task. Supported by his fanatical followers and by a courageous fighting force, the dreaded 'jagunços', he inflicted one defeat after another on the federal forces sent against him, which were out-manoeuvred and ambushed in the rugged, parched terrain 200 miles north of Salvador, and only succeeded in crushing his forces in a fourth and final expedition in 1897. The events of the campaign, the exploits and last-ditch bravery of the Counsellor's

[1] J. M. Bello, *A History of Modern Brazil,* p. 150.

men were told by Euclides da Cunha in 'Os Sertões' (The Backlands), a classic of Brazilian literature.

Another leader of a very different stamp, followed by the simple, credulous people of the sertão, was their great idol and miracle-worker, Father Cicero, a contemporary of the Counsellor but who lived on until 1934 as the father of the poor, the absolute ruler of Juàzeiro do Norte, a town in the interior of Ceará that became a centre of pilgrimage and a thriving commercial centre in his lifetime. He had originally gone there as a parish priest in the 1870s but soon found that he had to turn his hand to everything. In the severe droughts at the end of the decade, 'he distinguished himself and earned the deepest gratitude of the sertanejos by having wells dug, shelters constructed and fields of manioc planted. With such measures, he saved the lives of large numbers of refugees. His fame spread throughout the length and breadth of the sertão'.[1]

Later, Father Cicero's 'miracles' were joyfully accepted and skilfully promoted on his home-ground. Church commissions of inquiry, including doctors co-opted for the purpose, came to Juàzeiro to examine the evidence but produced conflicting reports; the sertanejos, however, remained unshaken in their convictions and noted with satisfaction that some of the clergy who had voted against Father Cicero suffered serious misfortunes. The 'miracles' finally got the Father into trouble with Rome, which unfrocked him, but he then concentrated on politics and came to terms with the dominant local party, which granted him authority over the backlands. Having become a powerful figure in Ceará, he went on to win national recognition and prestige. In his lifetime he commanded the services of a small private army; his name became a legend in the North-East and even today there are still sertanejos who prophesy the return of this apostle to the town that he made famous.

A region in decline

If today the North-East still bears marks of feudalism and backwardness, one should not forget that it was once the most dynamic, populous region of Brazil, and in the 1870s contained just under half of the total Brazilian population. In the early part of the colonization, the Portuguese concentrated on its development, establishing the sugar-cane plantations that

[1] T. Lynn Smith, *Brazil: People and Institutions,* pp. 553-4.

brought wealth to the metropolitan country and enhanced the colony's value. From the eighteenth century onwards, the North-East began to decline. With the discovery of gold in Minas Gerais and later the coffee boom in São Paulo, the economic axis of Brazil moved to the Centre-South, where it remained. The North-East was left to fend for itself, receiving close federal attention only when a North-easterner was elected President of Brazil or when some natural disaster, a drought or floods, inflicted such hardship on the region that sympathies in the South were aroused and the government was forced to alleviate the sufferings of the population.

When in the late nineteenth and the twentieth centuries the Centre-South industrialized and developed apace, the North-East was confined to the production and export of a colonial-type range of agricultural raw materials—the cotton of Pernambuco and Ceará, the sugar of Pernambuco and Alagoas, the cocoa of Bahia, the sisal of Bahia and Pernambuco, the vegetable oils of Ceará and Bahia, as well as a variety of tropical cereals, the cultivation of which was scattered throughout the region. Only the discovery of petroleum in Bahia, where the Brazilian oil industry came to be centred, modified this picture. Such manufacturing industry as the North-East possessed was modest and over-shadowed by the industries of the Centre-South, established on a much larger scale, while even the importance of the region's agriculture was threatened by the more efficient, abundant production of São Paulo and Paraná.

A poor region, where today the average yearly income is about £68 (170 dollars) per head, under half the Brazilian average, with the rural populations in the poorer states like Piauí living in African or Indian-style poverty, the North-East has long provided the great pool of unskilled labour for the rest of the country. The dustman in Rio, the factory worker at the Volkswagen plant outside São Paulo, the charwoman in the city apartment, the worker in the construction firm building roads across Brazil, is very often a North-easterner, from any of the nine states.

North-easterners went in their thousands to Amazônia to join in the rubber boom at the beginning of the century and they were among the 'candangos', the labour force that built Brasília over a decade ago. Migration to the Centre-South has been the escape-valve both for the educated North-easterner anxious to better himself, and for the illiterate labourer, driven out of the region by poverty, ruthless landlords or the drought. Brazilian literature is rich in stories of the dire conditions under which North-eastern peasants and their families have undertaken the long journey south, their plight often exploited by unscrupulous middlemen, who at times sold these people into little better than slavery.

In its remoteness from the developing Centre-South and particularly from Rio de Janeiro, until recently the seat of the federal government, the basic problems of the North-East seem to have commanded only sporadic attention or effective action from governments and politicians. Money and engineering skills were periodically put into attempts to tackle the recurrent drought problem by building reservoirs, which were of some benefit but were not complemented by rational systems of irrigation.[1]

One waits until the 1950s for the first authentic offorts to look at the North-eastern problem as one of under-development rather than of the cussedness of nature, which at irregular intervals denied parts of the region adequate rainfall. The setting up of the Bank of the North-East and the building of a large power station at the Paulo Afonso falls on the great, 2,400-mile River São Francisco were two important steps in this direction, and in 1959 came an imaginative proposal for a comprehensive attack on North-eastern problems; this was put forward to President Kubitschek by an economist, Celso Furtado, and was entitled 'An economic development policy for the North-East'.

The drought had struck again in 1958. With a growing realization that the North-East could not simply go on as it had for centuries, the Kubitschek administration put on the statute books a law to set up the Superintendency for North-eastern Development (Sudene). Naming this new approach the 'Operation North-East', Kubitschek was once again careful to instill a sense of drama into the whole project; he also appointed Furtado, a North-easterner from Paraíba, head of the new agency.

The new approach

In the official language, the task of Sudene was to lay down guide-lines for North-eastern development, to oversee and co-ordinate the carrying out of development projects in the

[1] Special budgetary funds were earmarked for public works in a large area, the 'drought polygon', defined by law in 1936 and expanded in 1947 and 1951.

region and to supervise national or foreign technical assistance programmes.

Set up late in 1959, Sudene was the executor of federal policy for the region and its Superintendent reported either to the Presidency, with direct access to the President, or to a federal ministry. In practice, Sudene, as a regional planning agency, came to dominate the whole development process in the North-East, ensuring that public investments were co-ordinated, channelling private investment into the region and striving to give the process coherence and direction through its successive multi-annual 'master plans' (planos diretores). It also provided means by which international and foreign agencies advised on, and participated in, tackling some of the problems that the region faced.

Sudene started its life with the opposition of the vested interests of the North-East, the traditional elites, the landowners, the politicians serving them and particularly the federal agencies already operating in the region, of which the Department of Works against the Drought (DNOCS) was the most determined in its antagonism. Its establishment was resisted by all who saw the emergence of a new power-centre, dedicated to the task of changing the economic and social face of the North-East, as a threat to the status quo, likely to interfere with their own position. In promulgating the law on Sudene, President Kubitschek said that he was fully aware of the existence of interests hostile to the government's initiative in launching the 'Operation North-East'. He had found obstacles to the new policy for North-eastern development, simple because the chronic state of abandonment of part of the Brazilian family had fostered a sort of industry, leading to greedy trafficking in the service of interests frequently contrary to those of the people and the administration.

There were nevertheless allies for the new agency. Those in the Centre-South who cared for and knew about the North-East, had for long been critical of the inefficiency and at times downright dishonesty of the administration of money and supplies sent for relief purposes to the region; they wanted to see a responsible body established to take on the overall problem. In this, they were joined by the Roman Catholic Church, especially by the North-eastern bishops, who publicly endorsed the proposal to set up Sudene and were to play an active part in promoting community projects and preaching the need for development of the region's human and material resources. The Sudene was also to

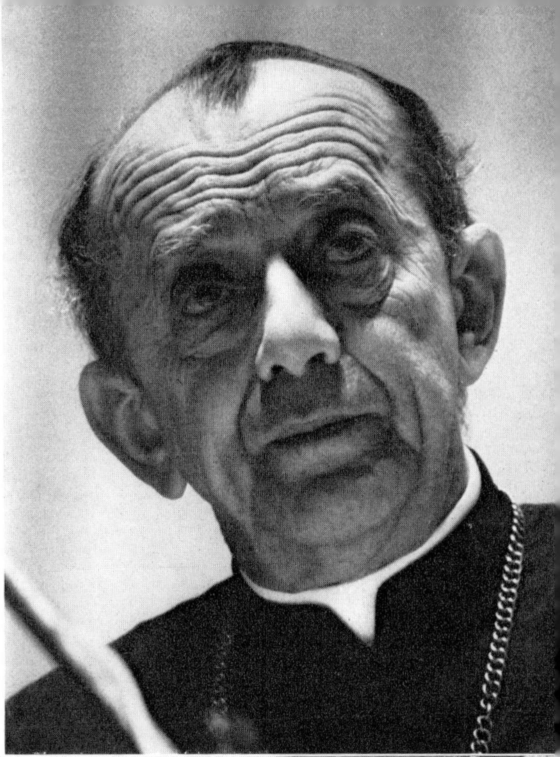

20 Dom Helder Câmara, Archbishop of Recife and Olinda

21 'Seventy per cent of the people live below the level of existence. They lack homes, land, everything'—Father Melo on the North-eastern problem

22 Power for the North-East: the Paulo Afonso Hydro-electric station

23 Agriculture in Pernambuco still uses the old, traditional methods

24 North-easterners work on an army-organized 'labour front' during the drough

25 President Kubitschek outside the Palace in Brasília

26 Lúcio Costa, 'town-planner' of Brasília

27 Oscar Niemeyer (right), in the drawing-office

28 The Congress

29 The 'crown of thorns' dome of Brasília Cathedral

30 The Foreign Office building, floodlit and reflected in its surrounding water

31 Claudio Vilas-Boas shares a boat on the Xingu river with a Txukarrainai Indian. The latter, in the tradition of his tribe, has his lower lip distended by the insertion of a plaque

32 Claudio talks with the people of one of the remote villages in the Xingu; they are of the Juruna tribe

33 December 1968: Paratroopers survey the remains of Father Calleri's expedition to pacify the Atroari Indians

34 While the machine prepares the road across Amazonia, the peasant leads the traditional 'beast of burden'

receive the support of the U.S.A. which, in its reaction to events in Cuba, was anxious to support action to help an obviously critical area.

The nature of the forces ranged against Sudene in its early years was probably decisive in determining the course that it was for long to follow almost exclusively—the creation of a dynamic industrial sector.[1]

From the viewpoint of Sudene, any attempt to take comprehensive action in the agrarian sector would be tenaciously opposed by the landowners, who dominated local politics and administration. The Sudene effort was therefore directed towards industrial development, which was much less likely to stir up political problems, would respond more quickly to a programme of federal incentives and would profit from the new power supplies from Paulo Afonso. Industrial development would, it was expected in the early days, help to alleviate the serious unemployment and under-employment problem in the urban areas, which was usually around the 1m. mark during the decade of the '60s.

Furthermore, it was expected that the emergence of a genuine industrial sector intended to supply the North-Eastern market, would provide a stimulus to the development of the region as a whole. In carrying out its programme for industrial development which, after a slow start in the early '60s, got under way and was progressively built up under Castello Branco and Costa e Silva, Sudene assisted the reorganization and expansion of existing enterprises, the rationalization of the ailing textile industry being a particular example. More importantly, however, it acted as the 'midwife' for the initiation of new industrial projects.

The means found to bring industry to the North-East sprang from a successfully operated scheme, typically Brazilian in its ingenuity and based on a system of incentives to private enterprise. The scheme's main feature was a federal concession enabling Brazilian or foreign firms established in the country, when paying income tax, to deduct up to 50 per cent of their tax liabilities and deposit the amount with the Bank of the North-East for subsequent investment in development projects approved by Sudene; the depositor could use the funds in his own project or invest them in the projects of others. The concession was

[1] In 1971, the government announced that priority would in future be given to agriculture rather than to industry.

liberalized and expanded in 1963. From 1964-5, with the advent of firm government under Castello Branco, the money available, known as '34/18 money' (from two articles in the Sudene legislation) increased considerably, as the big companies in the Centre-South, particularly in São Paulo, began to participate actively. The scheme was complemented by a wide range of facilities, including tax exemptions for the new firms established in the North-East, duty-free imports of equipment, financing with 'soft loans', technical assistance in the preparation of projects and purchase of land at nominal prices.

The 34/18 money was the principal means by which Sudene undertook its 'big push' in the industrial sector. Thus, in a summing up of ten years of activity, published by Sudene from its Recife headquarters in 1969, it claimed the approval of 721 industrial projects said to have brought about substantial changes in the structure of North-eastern industry, and to have contributed to the lessening of the serious unemployment problem in the region. The projects when completed would give direct employment to some 130,000 workers; assuming that each job directly created would lead to the creation of three other jobs in the regional economy, the total number of jobs created by private investments in industry would exceed half a million, Sudene said.

The industrialization programme presented a contribution, but by no means a solution to the unemployment problem. It was argued that the new factories, if they were to establish themselves, had to be based on modern equipment and methods, maintaining their labour force at levels that would keep their costs competitive. This was true enough, but more could perhaps have been done in selecting industrial activities that would be more labour-intensive.

The programme inevitably had its problems. At times, money seemed to pile up in the Bank of the North-East, reflecting a bottleneck in Sudene's processing and approval of projects and a slowness in the release and expenditure of the funds that flowed to the North-East.

Looking at the whole range of Sudene projects, there were bound to be doubts as to the proportion of them that in the future would prove able to stand on their own feet. From the taxpaying firm's angle, this was money that it would otherwise lose to the government anyway and under these conditions one must wonder if, in putting money into a Sudene project, as much care was exercised as in a normal investment. In the case of Sudene, there was a danger that, in the desire to press on with the development of the North-East, unsound criteria might be adopted in vetting the applications for projects received by the agency from North-Eastern or other businessmen; Sudene Superintendents were naturally at pains to stress that all projects were rigorously screened. In the case of North-eastern firms receiving the money there was also the danger, not to be overlooked in happy-go-lucky Brazil, that the businessman, less responsible than some, might use it not for investment but to pay off his debts or buy a new Ford Galaxie.

There was, however, encouragement for North-easterners in the new industrial areas on the roads leading out of Recife and in the handsome, spacious industrial estate of Aratu, outside Salvador, one of the really promising developments in the North-eastern scene. Nevertheless, the concentration of new projects in these two big cities and in Fortaleza, where industry found the favourable conditions of market and infrastructure lacking elsewhere in the region, aroused fears in the poorer states that a new, more prosperous North-East, composed of a few richer states, was coming into being and that they would remain among the 'have-nots'.

Another problem exercising Sudene's planners was whether the production from the new factories would be supported by steady expansion of the North-eastern market. Those who looked at its current limited size were doubtful on this score; they were the more inclined to pessimism when they looked at the backward state of agriculture and at the large number of people living at or below the subsistence level, not only in the sertão but in the more fertile areas. The prospects for these people becoming partners in a new, expanding market for North-eastern industry did not look promising.

In 1965 the system of incentives was extended to include investment in agriculture; by 1970, some 200 projects were under examination by Sudene, 90 per cent of them in cattle-raising. In 1969, it had set up its own seed production unit in Pernambuco. Nobody in the North-East had much difficulty in diagnosing the sick state of agriculture, the poverty of the rural populations being only too apparent, even to a superficial examination. There was inadequate use of land, with small properties using too much labour, and large, under-cultivated estates using too little; inefficient marketing and distribution largely in the hands of grasping middlemen, excessive supplies of cheap labour that discouraged the adoption of more rational methods of cultivation, added to a lack of investment. Here too, Sudene was urgently needed. The task of improving farming in the North-East could not be left to the small farmers, some of whom were destitute and under-nourished, nor to the big landowners, who mostly lived in the cities and were not too concerned about these problems.

Sclerosis in the sugar industry

In their world-wide drive to expand trade with their new colonial areas, the Portuguese began early to establish plantations in Pernambuco and throughout the long North-eastern coastal area, for the cultivation of cane and the export of sugar to Portugal. Workmen from Madeira and Jews fleeing from persecution in Portugal were believed to have built the first small sugar-mill of Pernambuco in 1534.[1] Others followed suit and the business proved profitable. Europe was clamouring for sugar, regarding it as a luxury and prepared to pay high prices for even unrefined brown sugar. However, the successful development of the sugar business in Brazil attracted the envy of the Dutch, who under John Maurice of Nassau invaded and occupied Pernambuco from 1630 to 1654; finally driven out of their New Holland in the tropics, they took their expertise and experience won in Brazil to the Caribbean, where they set up in highly successful competition.

The Portuguese implanted in the North-East a form of rural aristocracy in which the landowner exercised patriarchal authority over his household and the slave labour working on the plantation. This had its own characteristic framework: the big house (casa grande) of the owner and family with their negro servants, the slave-quarters (senzala) and the mill and cane-growing areas, which were often extensive. Ruling this domain with absolute authority, the owner controlled the life of the plantation in all its aspects, including the spiritual.[2]

At the chapel adjoining the big house, the rites of birth, death and marriage on the plantation were celebrated; if this had not already been done in Africa, newly-arrived slaves had to be baptized Christians before they were considered fully to be

[1] A. Tamer, *O Mesmo Nordeste,* p. 7.

[2] G. Freyre, *The Masters and the Slaves,* p. 197.

human beings. The plantation chaplain played his part in ensuring that the position of authority of the master, the 'senhor de engenho', was understood and respected, officiating and giving the blessing on the day when cane-grinding started. Slaves were fully instructed in the new faith, with the images of selected saints painted black for the purpose, but there was generally indulgence for the slaves' addiction to the customs and beliefs brought from their African homes, to the celebration of their festivals, to their dances and the preservation of their folklore.

Plantation discipline could be harsh and ruthless, however, especially for runaway slaves, and this discipline throughout the centuries was the strength of the plantation society, based on a well-knit aristocratic rural elite with a strong community of interests and a conservatism resistant to change. In its heyday, it was, by the standards of those times, an affluent society, living off sugar and the negro. It was also one that endured, changing little; not until the nineteenth century did it suffer its first great upheaval.

Brazil abolished slavery in 1888, shaking the foundations of the plantation system that had formed the basis of the North-eastern economy. The advent of the larger type mills, involving a more industrial approach to sugar production, also brought new methods of cane cultivation and, for a time, an increase in workers' wages. Any social benefits were apparently short-lived, however. Gilberto Freyre described the new situation in the twentieth century as follows:

> The slave's place was taken by the pariah of the factory, the slave hut was replaced by slums and the plantation master by the factory-owner and absentee capitalist. Many Big Houses remained closed, with the big estate-owners roaming about in automobiles from city to city, living in Swiss chalets and Norman Villas and finding diversion in Paris with ladies of easy virtue.[1]

The old society broke up, and the sugar companies inherited its power.

Of great impact on the fortunes of the industry was the arrival of the waves of European immigrants in the Centre-South of Brazil in the twentieth century, bringing with them a capital of knowledge and skills that were to be used, amongst other things,

[1] Ibid, p. lv.

in sugar production. The centre of gravity of the sugar industry now moved south to the state of São Paulo, where management proved more progressive than in the North-East, the terrain was better suited to mechanization and the whole industry was more productive. The North-eastern industry was hard hit by the slump of 1929, and was from then on to be a source of anxiety, with inevitable effects on the life of the masses of North-easterners who depended on it. Propped up by governmental protection, the industry also received in the late 1950s an unexpected shot in the arm from Fidel Castro's quarrel with the Americans, which led to their refusal to buy Cuban sugar and enabled the North-East to ship larger quantities to the lucrative American market.

With this stimulus added to the steady increase in sugar consumption that had been taking place in Brazil, the sugar companies of the North-East, in whose hands landownership in the fertile Zona da Mata was now concentrated, reached out to bring more land under cane cultivation and increase output. They absorbed more and more of the small plots of land available to the labourers, particularly to the seasonal worker, for the crops of maize, beans and manioc that they planted around their huts. Much of this land was less suitable for cane-growing than the land normally used and its appropriation, if it raised the companies' production, increased their average costs. The workers found their food supplies and their already wretched wages reduced as the companies cut their outlays.

Because of its economic and social conditions, the sugar belt of Pernambuco would strike most outside observers as a potential breeding-ground for unrest and agitation. The mills and plantations worked at full pressure only from September to March, during which time the cane was harvested, and then many of the workers were laid off, some being kept on at reduced pay to maintain the land and the equipment. Like the 'senhores de engenho', the mill and plantation-owners wielded virtually absolute powers over the workers; paternalism and servility were the keynotes of their relationship.[1] Labour was in surplus and wages low. Indeed, the workers often received not money but credit to obtain goods at the plantation store, the 'barracão', where they paid the owner's prices. Dues for the workers' organization, the

[1] Fanny Mitchell, 'Trouble in the Zona da Mata', Institute of Current World Affairs, New York, 1967.

'sindicato', were deducted from the pay packet by the employer, who did not always pass them on. Work and earnings could be easily controlled and adjusted by a task system, through which the employer laid down the amount of work to be done for a fixed sum.

The further deterioration of their living conditions in the 1950s made the cane-workers, illiterate and politically unorganized, ready for once to follow those wishing to influence them. In the late '50s and early '60s, the Zona da Mata was the scene of attempts by various groups to organize the workers in a struggle against the cane-planters and mill-owners. The incident that set the chain of events in motion occurred in 1955, when peasant-farmers on a former sugar-plantation west of Recife, the Engenho Galiléia, decided to form their own association and co-operative, and succeeded in resisting the attempts of the owner to evict them. In defending their interests, Francisco Julião, a local lawyer and Socialist party politician, went on to organize the Peasant Leagues (Ligas Camponesas) the first to stir up opposition to the mill and plantation-owners and to attempt to create a political consciousness among the workers.

The next to act was the Roman Catholic Church, which through the North-eastern bishops awoke to the need for action to improve the living conditions of the peasantry. In 1961, under the leadership of the reformist Bishop of Natal, Dom Eugênio Sales, they met and decided to provide an alternative to the movement of Julião, whose motives they mistrusted. As agitation began to grow in the sugar belt, two churchmen, Father Paulo Crespo and Father Antônio Melo, both North-easterners, undertook the task of organizing rural workers' trade unions.

They were men of contrasting personality and methods. Father Crespo, who headed the 'Rural Orientation Service' of Pernambuco, was a moderate, quiet in his manner, judicious in his actions, convinced that the ends could eventually be achieved within the law, by patient, persistent effort and work, helping the peasants to help themselves. Experience, however, made him well aware of the pervasive power of the 'system' and its inflexible opposition to organized labour in any form. Father Melo was impulsive and quick-tempered, with a sharp tongue that he was prepared to use on anyone, from the highest to the lowest, believing that more forceful methods should be adopted and that action should be taken right up to the limit of the law or even to its very brink. He had no illusions about the mill and plantation-owners and no confidence in the government; he believed that the peasants must be made to fight for themselves.[1]

The two men set to work in the teeth of hostile employers and bitter Communist competition, of various forms of intervention by the Pernambuco state government under Miguel Arraes, and by the federal government of President Goulart, anxious to profit by the workers' support. It was a period of ferment and confusion, in which some certainly wished to help the workers (the Catholic unions, for example), but many, in the Brazilian fashion, were out to derive the maximum advantage for themselves.

There were strikes and clashes between workers and employers. At some plantations, the hammer and sickle was hoisted over the administration offices and the owners were barred from entry to their property; the Communist union leaders prevented Father Crespo from entering his parish outside Recife. The federal government decreed a rural workers' statute, which increased the minimum wage, and there was a general strike of rural workers late in 1963 which wrung some concessions from the mill and plantation-owners, who for the first time felt the taste of physical danger. What would have emerged from this confused situation if its development had been allowed to continue unchecked, nobody was to know; but almost inevitably, at the end of it all, the workers had gained little or nothing. The outbreak of the military coup on March 31st 1964 cut short the whole process of agitation.

Groping for a solution

In restoring law and order and respect for private property in the North-East, the Movement of March 1964 made a clean sweep of all the left-wing oriented unions and agencies that had been active in the region, imprisoning some of their leaders, others having quickly left the area. The Church-sponsored federation of rural workers, after rigorous scrutiny, was allowed to pursue its activities under close supervision, suffering the opposition of the mill-owners and cane-planters, who, with their control of local politics and the police force, were well placed to harass the federation and its members by the various means at their disposal, including violence.

[1] Fanny Mitchell, 'Padre Crespo and Padre Melo: two approaches to reform', ICWA, New York, November 1967.

Meanwhile, as the economists and planners of the post-1964 regimes looked for the solution to the problems of the sugar industry, objective evidence of the situation among the families of the workers in the Zona da Mata began to come from a source, whose findings, based on scientific observation, could not be shrugged off by anybody in the North-East, whatever their political or economic interests. This source was the Institute of Nutrition of the Federal University of Pernambuco, headed by Dr. Nelson Chaves.[1]

In its work upon the growing problem of malnutrition in the North-East, the Institute's investigations revealed alarming facts, the existence of which had been suspected but which had never been spelled out clearly; hunger in the North-East had for so long, for decades and even perhaps centuries, been regarded as a commonplace. The Institute's teams paid particular attention to the Zona da Mata where population was comparatively dense, carrying out a study in depth at Ribeirão, south of Recife. The studies concluded that in the southern sector of the Zona da Mata in Pernambuco, 70 per cent of the children in the pre-school age group were undernourished and 20 per cent seriously undernourished, owing to chronic deficiencies in the family diet, seriously lacking in proteins, minerals and vitamins. The situation of children from one to four years old was particularly serious; prematurely weaned, they were subject to all the dangers inherent, at that age, in a grossly inadequate diet. The effects on the children concerned were both physical and mental, and unless action was taken to remedy this situation, there would in the future be thousands of people in the North-East with retarded mental development.

Speaking to the author in Recife, Dr. Chaves attributed this situation to the economic and social conditions of the North-East, including the difficulties in the sugar industry. Starting in 1967, the Institute and the Health Department of Pernambuco, later with the support of the Church and the Special Group for Rationalization of the Sugar Industry (Geran), began to set up in the region centres of nutritional recovery—there were now five—to which the mothers could bring the children most seriously affected for periods of recovery, when the children were restored by a planned diet and the mothers received instruction to enable them to make better use of the food actually available in the

[1] See *O Mesmo Nordeste,* A. Tamer, p. 105.

region. There had initially been some resistance to the idea of these centres by the mill-owners, and lack of interest elsewhere, Dr. Chaves said, but the work done by Father Crespo and Father Melo in the region had contributed to making people more alert to the situation. There had even been recently evidence of a change of attitude among employers; the Estreliana mill in the sugar belt had agreed to the setting up of a nutritional centre on the plantation, a sign that some modification of mentality was taking place.

Of the North-eastern workers generally, the Institute found that the average level of their calorie intake was well below the average for all Brazil, their diet being seriously short of protein. According to studies carried out at Palmares, another town to the south, the average daily calorie intake had dropped to under 1700.[1] Although the working day was of eight hours, absenteeism was 40 per cent, reducing the effective working time to four or five hours per day. The area of land cultivated by a worker in the sugar belt of Pernambuco was scarcely half of what could be done by a labourer of São Paulo; the same situation applied in the cutting of sugar-cane.

Typical workers in the Zona da Mata were thin and short, predisposed to infection, with low work capacity, and grew old before their time; practically all of them were suffering from worms and intestinal parasites. Father Crespo described the workers' situation to the author by the phrase: 'They are dying little by little' ('Estão morrendo aos poucos'). Dr. Chaves would not go quite as far as that, but put it in more professional terms, by saying that their metabolism adapted to life at a lower level and they worked little; otherwise, how could they survive?

What was the solution for the sugar industry in the North-East? So many depended on it—in Pernambuco alone about 170,000 workers were employed on the 42 sugar plantations and mills and the whole industry, the most important in the North-East, employed around 450,000 people in some 104 properties. Over 400 years old, the industry was creaking with age. In the economists' language of Sudene, it was a 'monoculture' and had practically monopolized the use of the agricultural land in the Zona da Mata (black soils well suited to the growing of various

[1] Labourers in the sugar belt would need a daily calorie intake of 2,500, according to information quoted by A. Tamer, in *O Mesmo Nordeste*.

tropical products) and had established a form of agrarian organization unable to pay the populations tied to it income that would make them a genuine consumer market. Its internal vices and its excessive dependence on markets overseas or outside the region accounted for its inability to save and invest. It was devoid of vitality and excessively vulnerable.

The conclusions of the post-1964 regime's planners, backed by the opinion of local North-eastern experts, were: increase productivity in the cane-growing areas and at the mills; cut down the area of land planted with cane, and free land for food production and the raising of the living-standards of the workers.

The blueprints prepared by the federal government, from President Castello Branco onwards (who was a North-easterner and well aware of the seriousness of the problem) were drawn up on this basis, with all the necessary elaboration. The Special Group for Rationalization of the Sugar Industry (Geran), set up in 1966, revived again late in 1968 and finally abolished in 1971 after having achieved little, produced technically admirable studies and solutions that never got off the ground in Pernambuco, although in Alagoas, the second producing state in the North-East, there was a more progressive outlook and readiness to co-operate fully.

The industry had many-sided problems. Unable to compete with São Paulo, it suffered its own pricing problems, even though North-eastern sugar received protection (with almost exclusive access to the regional market), and was granted preference in exports to the lucrative American market. Suffering a sharp squeeze from 1962 onwards, first owing to uncontrolled inflation and then to the policies of retrenchment followed by governments after 1964, many of the mill and plantation-owners came to live off the Bank of Brazil which consolidated and then reconsolidated their debts.

The worst problem lay elsewhere, however. With some exceptions (and the author visited one of these at São José), the industry suffered from owners living in the past, who had failed utterly to bring to it modern, responsible capitalism. Fearing the consequences of the inevitable economic and, above all, social changes that would result from the implementation of schemes to rationalize the industry, many of them were only too reluctant to be dragged into the twentieth century.

Drought-scourge of the North-East

Euclides da Cunha, in his account of life in the backlands, saw the drought as 'the utmost terror of the countryman' and described the struggle of the sertanejos in 'the land's rebellion against man', telling in dramatic terms the ordeal of flight as the drought drove them from their homes.[1]

The sertão receives its rain not in the winter and from the Atlantic, as do the other North-eastern areas, but in the summer from the unreliable weather-fronts moving in from Maranhão or from the south. The high rate of evaporation and the geological conditions of the area, not favouring the retention of water, add to the problem. Rainfall in a normal year may average some 30 inches for the whole of the sertão, but there is a long strip of much lower rainfall extending northwards from northern Bahia through Pernambuco and Paraíba to Rio Grande do Norte, which acts as a kind of division between the rains coming from the Atlantic and those that develop from the continental fronts.[2]

Often uncertain in the time of its occurrence, rain in the sertão can be brief and violent, erupting in heavy downpours. When, however, the rains hold off month after month, the plantings fail and the wells and streams begin to dry up, leaving no water for the cattle; then the people of the sertão, however attached they may be to their land, have to leave for the coast or the south to seek food, water and work. It is the familiar story of the refugee (the 'flagelado' or 'retirante') taking to the paths and roads and begging for food on the way, well told in Cabral de Melo Neto's *Morte e Vida Severina* ('Death and Life of Severino'), the tragedy of the refugee who, driven from the backlands by the drought, left a life of privation but found nothing in the city of the coast.

There have always been droughts in the North-East, and Euclides recorded them as occurring in 9 to 12 year cycles. In one of the worst, in 1877, some 500,000 people were said to have perished from starvation and disease, and the Emperor Dom Pedro II ordered the chartering of ships, to take the unfortunate refugees off to colonize Amazônia, as well as the building of reservoirs to store water, against future emergencies. The worst droughts, which at times led to violence as the refugees broke into food-stores and looted shops, were accompanied by public

[1] In *Os Sertões* (The Backlands) mentioned above.

[2] Celso Furtado, *Diagnosis of the Brazilian crisis,* pp. 151-2.

sympathy in the South and by emergency relief measures, followed by federal programmes to build dams, reservoirs and roads to strengthen the region's defences. There were often abuses in the handling of the federal funds coming in to the distressed areas, with the unscrupulous stealing relief food-supplies and making money from the refugees' misfortunes, creating in the process the so-called 'drought industry', investigated, usually without much result, by commissions of inquiry.

In 1958 under President Kubitschek and again in 1970 during the Médici administration the droughts were severe and by then many had become convinced that the drought problem must be tackled from the viewpoint of the overall development of the region.

The effects of the drought of 1970 began to reach crisis proportions during May and June, and they were widespread. Among the states hardest hit were Ceará, Rio Grande do Norte and Paraíba, from where there were reports of groups of refugees assaulting food-stores and warehouses.

Once again, federal and state relief measures, co-ordinated by Sudene, went into action, with the armed forces called upon to play their part, through the shipment of emergency supplies into the region by the Navy and Air Force and through the organization of the 'labour fronts', particularly by the Army's engineering battalions, which joined Sudene in setting up the public works tasks in which the peasants were occupied. These men received food rations with a small token wage—2 cruzeiros (14 new pence) per day—and worked on building roads or reservoirs, leaving on Fridays for their homes and families, which might be as much as 40 miles away, and returning to the camps on Sundays to start the next week's work. At the height of the drought, nearly 500,000 men with a total of 2.5m. dependants were employed in some 150 'work fronts'.[1]

For the first time in history, a President of the Republic visited the drought areas and saw for himself the extent of the problem. A programme of irrigation in selected North-eastern areas was later announced by the Médici administration.

In this sector United Nations, French and Israeli technical missions had been working with the Brazilians in the North-East to build up existing knowledge on the extent of the underground

[1] Peter Oakley, 'Small-scale development in the North-East', *Bolsa Review*, London, October 1971, p. 577.

water resources and on the possibilities of irrigation in agriculture. It was a big problem, in the solution of which little real progress had been made.

'We are making little drops in this huge country', Aminadav Eilat, head of the Israeli technical co-operation mission, told the author in Recife. Speaking of one of the Israeli-run irrigation projects in Piauí, he wryly commented that the daily flow of water in the river there, the Parnaíba, was equivalent to the entire volume of water used in Israel in a year. Another Israeli technician was reported as saying: 'If we had one river like the São Francisco, we should make not one, but five states of Israel'. As one stands on the bridge linking the twin towns of Petrolina and Juàzeiro, in the middle reaches of this powerful river, one wonders, as many Brazilians have done, whether it could be harnessed to beat the North-eastern drought problem. In this river valley, where the Suvale[1], Sudene and FAO were working on irrigation projects, experience and information were being won on the most suitable crops to be grown and on the possibilities of selling them in the North-East or outside the region. Meanwhile, a national irrigation plan had been drawn up by an Israeli and a Brazilian firm. In going for a full, technical solution in this field, Brazil had made a late start.

A will to progress

In the broader context, Sudene itself came late, as did the efforts made in the North-East to overcome long-standing problems. In the last decade, however, there have been encouraging signs. The North-eastern economy has begun to grow faster than that of Brazil as a whole, even though the region still has far to go before its people can enjoy an acceptable standard of living. Millions of North-easterners still have to feel the beneficial effects of the development that took place in the 1960s but some at least are now looking forward to the idea of a 'new North-East' becoming a reality—an essential step to keep North-easterners at home and stem the flow of migration to the South.[2]

Behind the official programmes and the building of roads, power-stations and telecommunications networks, the communities scattered over this large, sprawling region are stirring and

[1] Suvale: the Superintendency for the valley of the São Francisco.

[2] Peter Oakley, 'Resurgence of the North-East', *Financial Times,* London, December 17th 1971, p. 29.

trying to move forward to something better; the map of the North-East is becoming dotted with individual, often unco-ordinated attempts at improvement. There is much to be done to awaken and educate under-privileged North-easterners to play a part in a process of development and to take initiatives within it; but with luck, some day the region will shake off the legacy of backwardness inherited from its past.

9 The Other Brazil: Amazônia and the Centre West

The problem of Brasília

> Brazil has taken its destiny in its own hands, and our new capital will be a symbol of the rise of a great new civilization in the tropics.
>
> President Kubitschek[1]

> The city should be planned for orderly and efficient work, but should also be a lively, delightful city suitable for reverie and intellectual speculation, able to become in time the seat of government and administration, and one of the brightest cultural centres of the country.
>
> Lúcio Costa, author of the Pilot Plan for Brasília[2]

> As an instrument for development of the interior, Brasília seems to suffer from the initial error made in its location. This is a capital set down in the middle of a desert, which has created nothing around it except heavier air traffic.
>
> Mário Henrique Simonsen, economist[3]

Twelve years after its inauguration in 1960, Brasília was a source of national pride but also a debate and controversy.

The idea of building a new capital far in the interior to be named Brasília, is said to have been first publicly raised some 150 years ago, by José Bonifácio, the elder statesman and 'patriarch', on the eve of the proclamation of independence; there had already been some discussion of the need to move the capital inland on the grounds that the seat of government in Rio was too vulnerable to attack from the sea. The hiatus between discussion and action was to prove a wide one. During the nineteenth century decrees were issued, committees deliberated, articles were

[1] *Brasília,* Brazilian Government Trade Bureau, London, p. 39.

[2] *O Estado de São Paulo,* Suplemento de Brasília, April 1970, p. 5.

[3] Mário Henrique Simonsen, *Ensaios Sobre Economia e Política Econômica,* Apec Editôra, Rio, 1971, p. 127.

3a The Belém-Brasília highway

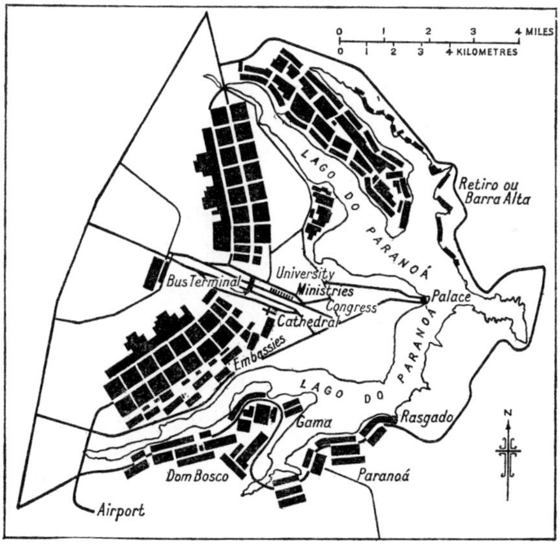

3b City-plan of Brasília

written in learned journals and the idea even found its way into the 1891 constitution, which set aside an area on the plateau of the Centre-West, in the state of Goiás.

Debate continued in the twentieth century and in 1922 the first foundation-stone was laid, as part of the celebrations of the centenary of independence. Further clauses were written into constitutions, Getúlio Vargas launched his 'Go West' campaign and a consensus formed on the location of the new capital in an area washed by tributaries of three major river basins, those of the Paraná, the São Francisco and the Tocantins (itself a tributary of the Amazon). The forces of inertia and the opposition of the political and commercial interests of Rio still had to be overcome, however, and this only happened in 1955 when Juscelino Kubitschek seized on the whole project during his presidential election campaign and, once in office, to everybody's surprise secured ready approval by Congress. A competition was launched and the President appointed an international panel, under Sir William (now Lord) Holford, to choose from among the designs submitted for the city; a construction agency was also set up.

Lúcio Costa won the award for the 'Pilot Plan'—the blueprint for the building of the city—and he was apologetic for the simplicity of his design, born 'of the elementary act of indicating a place or taking possession of it: two axes intersecting at right-angles in the sign of the cross'. To fit the local topography, however, Costa bent back the axis carrying the residential areas and the roads serving them, to make the shape of Brasília swept-wing, with the fuselage (the 'monumental axis') housing the political and administrative buildings, the Cathedral and the cultural centres. Where the axes intersected, he placed a spacious platform, on and around which were grouped the bus terminal, places of entertainment, office buildings and banks. For the residential areas, he introduced a system of 'super-blocks' ('superquadras'), each of eleven apartment-buildings, with children's playgrounds, schools, shops, lawns and trees. Brasília was, in Costa's concept, to possess all the attributes of a capital city and to be monumental, not in the sense of ostentation but of a consciousness of its worth and significance.

The second protagonist in this venture was Oscar Niemeyer, leader of a group of architects influenced by Le Corbusier and responsible for the post-war emergence of a modern Brazilian architecture that won international recognition for its vigour and inventiveness. The two men joined to create a city for 'a planned community under strict architectural control from the outset'.[1] This was a 'complete antithesis of the traditional Brazilian method of city development', which in the case of Rio and São Paulo had been expressed in a process of uncontrolled commercial enterprise'.

The work of supervising the construction, in which people from all over the country took part, was assigned to the Mineiro engineer and politician, Israel Pinheiro, under whom the work was pressed forward to meet the date fixed by President Kubitschek for the inauguration: April 23rd 1960.

The expense of the whole project and its rapid execution in three years was, both at the time and in later years, to create dissension. The building of the city, the critics argued, was undertaken before there were adequate all-weather roads or rail communications (the rail link to Pires do Rio, joining Brasília to São Paulo and Rio was only completed in March 1967) and many asserted that building materials had on occasions been flown in by air. This sort of extravagance, they claimed, gave a powerful stimulus to the rate of inflation, the rapid increase of which was a major factor in the downfall of the administrations following that of Kubitschek. They attributed his haste to complete the new capital during his term of office to Pharaonic self-promotion. Such charges he denied, but there was no doubt that he was extremely anxious to make the building of the city irrevocable.

The first decade of Brasília was marked by numerous 'ups and downs'. Established as a centre of government and part of a Federal District of 2,240 square miles, it depended on the federal government to earmark money yearly for its maintenance and expansion, and funds were all too often scarce. The city underwent periodic paralyses under Presidents Quadros and Goulart, suffering food and fuel crises and interruptions of its telephone communications, as a result of successive political upheavals and financial problems. The presence of Congress, then politically important, kept the city alive and commerce in being, thanks to the expenditure of federal deputies and senators and of the administrative staff. The evolution towards full capital city status was slow. Throughout the decade of the '60s, Brazil main-

[1] J. M. Richards, 'The architectural revolution in Brazil', in *Brasília*, Brazilian Government Trade Bureau, London.

tained two capitals, Brasília and Rio de Janeiro where the great mass of the machinery of government remained; the civil servants, particularly if they were Cariocas[1] used to the beaches and other attractions of Rio, resisted tenaciously the government's attempts to move them to what they considered to be a town isolated in the interior.

The military coup of 1964 brought a new phase to the life of the city. President Castello Branco was reported as saying that the building of Brasília was madness, but that to abandon it would be even greater madness. Whatever his strictures, however, he gave support and prestige to the city, appointing an able administrator, and despite the inevitable periods in Rio, spent much of his time there. So did President Costa e Silva, under whom the pace of building was stepped up and good administration continued. Then came, however, the period of Brasília's crisis—the depressing, dreary year that began with the issuing of the 5th Institutional Act in December 1968 and the closure of Congress, and ended with Costa e Silva's illness and government from Rio by the three military ministers. Brasília had even before 1969 begun to feel the impact of the decline in the prestige of Congress, which had been the mainspring of the city's existence. It passed through perhaps its blackest days during that year when business and commerce ground to a halt, the hotels were empty, bars and restaurants deserted and people moved out of the city with empty pockets.

It was left to General Médici, having assumed the Presidency, to revive activity in the city by insisting on his ministers being regularly available in Brasília and on the move of a central nucleus of the federal ministries and other agencies of government. This transfer of important elements of the Executive, which was to include the move of the Foreign Office (and ultimately of the foreign embassies), promised to replace the former dependence of the city on the Congress and to give it at last a badly-needed measure of stability. The high cost of bringing civil servants and their families to Brasília would, however, continue to impose a heavy financial burden on the Exchequer.

What of the life of the city, created to be the capital of the Republic? It was a city for the young, with children forming half of its population, a much greener city that had largely overcome the problem of the all-pervading red dust of its early years

[1] Carioca: a native of the city of Rio de Janeiro.

by planting grass and trees. Its dry air—the altitude was some 3,800 feet and the humidity low—gave it at times a rarefied atmosphere and the breadth of its sky conveyed a feeling of space. With new buildings being gradually added, there was delight for the eye in its architecture : the Congress buildings, the Planalto and Alvorada palaces, the Foreign Office, the Palace of Justice and the Cathedral; but there was monotony in the series of evenly spaced 'superquadras' and tedium in the way of life for many of those coming from Rio and São Paulo, who found it difficult to adjust. Outside the city, the countryside was bare and lacking in points of interest. Recreation found, however, a centre of activity in the artificial lake of Paranoá.

In a number of respects, the city had diverged from the aims of its inspired planner and architect, Lúcio Costa and Oscar Niemeyer, who saw it as a city to diminish class distinctions and social tensions, with people from all levels living in the same 'superquadras' and enjoying the same recreational facilities. Although all classes tended to share a pride in their city and to feel something of its original pioneering spirit, Brasília did not fulfil the ideals of its founders but began to reflect the realities and inequalities of Brazil as a whole. Niemeyer complained that it had become a city just like others, unjust and discriminatory. The Brasílienses, now some 546,000[1] coming from many of the states of the Republic, lived in distinct areas—congressmen, professional and businessmen in the superquadras of the Pilot Plan, tradespeople and skilled workers in the larger satellite towns of Taguatinga, Gama and Sobradinho, while the lower classes lived in a bustling slum area known as the Cidade Livre ('Free Town'), which had housed the labour force that built the city.

Despite these separations, typical of Brazil, and notwithstanding Niemeyer's comment, Brasília could never become a city 'just like others', even if the informal, accessible Brazilians were successful in placing their stamp upon this formal, aloof city. Its location in infertile country ill-suited for farming and, as Simonsen indicated, unlikely to have a life of its own, emphasized the functional nature of the task of national integration imposed upon it.

President Kubitschek saw Brasília as turning the attention of his countrymen away from the coastal regions to the interior and, in lofty language, spoke of a new era in which wealth and

[1] 1970 Census figures.

civilization would radiate out from the city to the heart of the country. More concretely, he believed that it would promote unity and that by removing government from the sectional interests and lethargic atmosphere of highly political Rio, it would improve the quality of administration.[1] Looking at the city in its initial stages, Sir William Holford wrote: 'A federal capital city near the centre of gravity of the country as a whole, lying between a rich agricultural region, an area of mineral resources, the hydro-electric capacity of the São Francisco valley, and the partially unexplored territories of the Mato Grosso, could act as a stable administrative centre, a string on which a great deal of sugar could crystallize'.[2]

In 1971 there were grounds for believing that some of these hopes might ultimately be fulfilled. Brasília had been successful in directing the thoughts of Brazilians to the hinterland but it could hardly be a source of wealth for the remainder of the country. To disseminate prosperity and economic progress was the role of already developed centres such as São Paulo, which possessed a capital of organization, knowledge and skills that the less-developed regions of the country urgently needed. Moreover, decades must pass before Brasília could form cultural resources comparable to those long owned by an older city like Rio.

In the functional tasks of fostering national integration, and of acting as an administrative centre, however, the prospects were better. Structural changes had been determined and were taking effect. Under the National Transport Plan, Brasília was now the centre of the land and air transport system and it was to become so for telecommunications. In a slow, painful process, Brasília was acquiring the importance as an administrative centre that Rio was losing, and a movement into the interior was gradually gaining momentum.

The level of expense involved in waiting for the full realization of these more specific hopes was however proving a burden. As Brasília, a drain on the national Treasury and an absorber of scarce resources, began its second decade, the problem was: when would the heavy investment made in building Brasília begin to pay off? Certainly not yet, it seemed, and it was difficult to tell when the balance-sheet would move out of the red into

[1] Richard Bourne, *Political Leaders of Latin America,* p. 185.

[2] 'The Pilot Plan: its qualities and objectives', in *Brasília,* Brazilian Government Trade Bureau, London, pp. 9-10.

the black. It was more likely to do so when the city became the centre in which all or most of the important national decisions were taken. In the current phase of Brazilian history, this would largely be decided by the armed forces.

Now it seemed that the Brazilian military, in pursuit of the objective of national security and defence of the frontiers, accepted Brasília as the convenient centre from which to deploy their forces and to develop their strategy of occupation of Brazil's wide open spaces in the Centre-West and, above all, in Amazônia. 'Because of new factors resulting from the transfer of the capital, the nucleus of Brazil, previously restricted to the Rio-São Paulo-Belo Horizonte triangle, is already expanding to include Brasília and form a quadrilateral containing the demographic and economic core of the country' said a leading spokesman for the Movement of March 1964.[1]

To the military, therefore, accustomed to the interior of the country and to frequent postings, Brasília would be a base for the process of national integration—a motel or transit camp on the way to Amazônia and the West.

The 'Belém-Brasília'

An integral part of the plan to transfer the federal capital to the plateau was the building of trunk-roads, linking it to the largest cities and principal regions of Brazil—to Rio and São Paulo, the North-East, the West, and the North. This bold scheme was an essential element in the efforts to consolidate the position of the inland capital. Thus, during the period of feverish activity that saw the building of the city, the Kubitschek administration drove a dirt-road some 1,350 miles long from Brasília to Belém, capital of the state of Pará and a port some 90 miles below the mouth of the River Amazon.

For a long time, governments had been trying to solve the problems of ending the isolation of the North and, in the absence of a proper shipping service, had tried various combinations of rail, road and river to join eastern Amazonas with the south. None of them made much headway—the river most suitable, the Tocantins, was 'cussed', like many Brazilian rivers; it was navigable for only limited stretches because of rapids, and the possibilities for economic solutions were restricted. Then developments

[1] General A. de Lyra Tavares, quoted in *O Estado de São Paulo,* April 18th 1970, p. 3.

within Brazil in the '50s, the establishment of motor vehicle production and the ready availability of heavy road-building equipment and oil products, made an all-road solution feasible.

Kubitschek found among the men working on Brasília a well-known pioneering figure to head the highway venture—Bernardo Sayão, an engineer who had been building roads in that part of the country and had always preached the need for a road link with Belém. He set to work in 1958 with several thousand workmen, 400 heavy tractors and teams working overtime at both ends of the projected route. Existing roads that Sayão himself had engineered were of some minor assistance and the men met the worst difficulties in pushing the road through the virgin tropical rain-forests of the North: they lit signal fires to show which part of the forest they had reached and food supplies were dropped by air to keep them going.[1] After some two years of hard labour, a 'pioneer road' was completed early in April 1960, in time for a convoy of Northerners to drive down it for the inauguration of Brasília later in the month.

Sayão himself did not live to see the completion, killed by a falling tree shortly before the northern team met the men working up from the south, but the 'Belém-Brasília' now bears his name, as the 'Rodovia Bernardo Sayão'. For some years, the road was only open during the dry season. Derided by political opponents of the Kubitschek regime as a 'track for wildcats', it fell to rack and ruin when he left the Presidency, being restored, however, from 1964 onwards and, with periodic setbacks, kept open for traffic throughout most of the year.

When the author made this journey in 1967, the bus left at 6 a.m. from the terminal in Brasília and it was some consolation to think that at the same uncivilized hour a load of south-bound passengers was also boarding a bus in Belém on the four-day journey. Our passengers: thrifty middle-class Brazilians, mostly bound for Belém, for whom the cheapness of the bus fare (costing the equivalent of only £4) was the primary consideration. One of them had an Amazonian island—a family heirloom—for sale and was anxious to find an American and hard currency. Two Peace Corps girls, laboratory technicians, after bus journeys covering a good part of Brazil, were returning to their base in Acre where they would continue researching into tropical diseases. 'You name it and we've got it,' was their comment on the range of ailments in their territory.

[1] Valverde and Vergolino Dias: *A Rodovia Belém-Brasília,* p. 331.

The vehicle was a standard product from the Mercedes-Benz factory in São Paulo and should, one thought, be durable enough, since it was the same type that suffered maltreatment from the negro bus-drivers in Rio, but seldom, from the author's experience, broke down. Later on in the journey, however, when a window fell out on top of the Peace Corps girls and a fuel pipe broke from the constant vibration, emptying all the diesel oil onto the road, one concluded that the 'Belém-Brasília' was more than a match for the products of industry. From this latter disaster, we were saved, as may happen in Latin American catastrophes, great or small, by the prompt aid of an American 'mission', providentially located back down the road!

Running up between two big rivers, the Araguaia and Tocantins, the road followed their watershed and cut through one of Brazil's most under-developed regions, containing the states of Goiás, Maranhão and Pará. From Brasília it first described a long loop to the south-west to take in Anápolis, a prosperous looking farming centre in S. Goiás, before turning north. The asphalt road, amidst plantations of rice, beans and maize in a green countryside, lasted only a few more miles and then came the dirt surface that was to be with us for a full three days until the asphalt reappeared just under 95 miles from Belém.

Until midday on the third day of the journey, the bus toiled up towards the northern border of Goiás and we passengers felt in our bones, during 12 hours a day, including stops for meals and 'cafèzinhos',[1] the endless time it could take to cross just one state in Brazil, with its truly continental dimensions. The country was of low trees and open scrub, savanna country, that gave space and pasture for cattle-raising. Many of the passing trucks were loaded with cattle from the ranches that were a dominant feature of the local economy, while the rest were usually heavy lorries with number plates from São Paulo, Minas, Paraná and Rio Grande do Sul carrying foodstuffs, manufactured goods and merchandise up north. The road was maintained by Rodobrás, a government agency, which was slowly rationalizing its engineering. Rodobrás aimed to keep the Belém-Brasília open throughout the rainy season and maintained communications through its district offices spaced out along the road; but the link was at times precarious.

Some sizeable towns had grown up along the road and some

[1] Cafèzinho: the small, sweet cups of Brazilian coffee.

old, decaying ones had taken on a new lease of life, like Imperatriz, which grew from 8,000 inhabitants to 70,000 in ten years. Everywhere there was change. Hamlets sprang up overnight, took root or suddenly vanished as people moved on. There were frequent villages, the life of which revolved around the long-distance traffic, with simple restaurants, filling stations, mechanics' 'shops', tyre-repairers and over-night stopping places with minimum standards of comfort and sanitation. Occasionally a cinema, a football field, a rough travelling circus, or even a primitive brothel for truck-drivers, provided recreation. At the hamlet of Pisa no Freio ('Step on the brake'), not far from the Goiás-Maranhão border, Dona Rita, the local hotel-owner, catered for the last-named trade. Two Brazilian journalists reported on her 'international' staff, claiming that she had a Japanese girl born in Amazônia, a Paraguayan and two French girls. The claim aroused scepticism among connoisseurs of the Belém-Brasília: Brazilian 'madams' have always seen the advantages to sales of teaching the girls a few words of French. Business was brisk at Dona Rita's—there was usually a long queue of heavy trucks outside the establishment, breaking the long journey through the night!

Despite such distractions, it was monotonous country, with a subsistence-type agriculture, and innumerable primitive, straw-thatched huts where the peasant eked out a simple and at times precarious livelihood, not venturing far in from the roadside. Our bus gave a local service to these people, picking them up, charging them a cruzeiro or two and dropping them off at the village of their destination. When the bus moved out of Goiás, over a splendid bridge 500 yards long, the eyes welcomed the sight of water, the broad expanse of the River Tocantins; we were already passing into Amazônia, with its heavy rainfall, tall trees and tropical vegetation. This again was cattle country, particularly in Pará, where were many of the cattle-ranching projects approved by the Superintendency for Amazonian Development (Sudam).

To the areas along the road had come the poor Northerners from Maranhão and Pará or North-easterners fleeing from the drought: herdsmen, prospectors, woodcutters, hunters and peasant farmers, with few resources and primitive methods of cultivation, looking for work and hungry for any land where they would be free from the rule of the landowner. Often their hopes were disappointed—the land-grabbers and speculators were a plague here, as elsewhere in Brazil—and they ended up working for the barest living in regions where the tropical diseases, malaria, verminosis and Chagas disease, took their toll. Where local raw materials encouraged industry and the spirit of initiative, however, the boom town appeared, as in Araguaina in Northern Goiás. Here the availability of mahogany, babaçu[1] and fertile land fostered the emergence of a fast-growing community, land values went up fast and the local stores, with a healthy pioneering smell of leather, stocked everything for the house, farm or business.

A journey made today would reflect the extent of migration inside Brazil. Ten years ago there were probably about 50,000; now there are said to be nearly two million people living along the Belém-Brasília, in what was in 1967 certainly an occupation but not, in the full sense of the word, a settlement of the territory. Having built the road, the federal authorities and, equally, the state governments, lacked the money and staff to follow this up with action to back firmly-based settlement. The migrants had to rely on their own resources, having to face the hardships inherent in such a life, often in the absence of eradication teams or disease control measures from ministries of health or other bodies. In the 1970s, government was at last making its presence felt in telecommunications, in the erection of the microwave towers that would link Belém and the towns along the highway by telegraph and telephone to Brasília and the developed areas of the Centre-South. One traveller reported that civilization, in the shape of TV transmissions of Brazil's World Cup victories in Mexico, had reached some towns along the Belém-Brasília!

Eastern Amazônia, behind its thick wall of forest, had for long lived in isolation, much as a colony separated from a metropolitan Brazil. In joining it to the Centre-South and above all to São Paulo, the Belém-Brasília won economic advantages for the present and the future. The 'colony' was ready for emancipation and integration. For the Belém businessmen and shopkeepers, the new road meant a door-to-door, if relatively expensive, delivery in a week or ten day of goods from the South that would have taken a month by ship, if they arrived at all. São Paulo could send north a regular flow of its new cars, iron and steel products, plastics and varied food-products, while the North

[1] Babaçu : a large palm-tree yielding oil, fibres and other products.

could send its pepper, timber and rubber, amongst other commodities. For the state of Goiás, which it formerly took many days to cross on horseback or by canoe, the road was a potential artery of development, from which in due course feeder roads would radiate into the interior.

The Belém-Brasília achieved above all a political objective, in making the Northerners feel that they were part of a country and not poor relations left to fend for themselves. The effects of this were shown in a new desire in the North, despite complaints about Paulista 'imperialism', to go ahead with development and to take a fresh look at the region's human and material resources.

A military obsession?

If the military men who governed Brazil from 1964 could be said to have an obsession, then it was the occupation of Amazônia.

By the mid-twentieth century Amazônia, as at present geographically defined, had been part of Brazil for three hundred years or more, and for Brazilians, in an often ill-defined manner, it was a symbol of national greatness and an assurance of an impressive future. It had enjoyed a period of world-class importance with the rubber boom that began in the 1890s and collapsed around 1914, after the British had developed production in Asia from seeds quietly removed from Brazil by a botanist, Henry Wickham. Amazônia enjoyed a short but golden era and in the national consciousness it then reverted to its normal status, of being a challenge but one requiring so much capital and effort that it should best be left to future generations with more resources to overcome the numerous obstacles that it presented. It was therefore largely left to its own devices while the Centre-South of Brazil went ahead with its own development.

By the 1960s there was increased international interest, in the United Nations specialized agencies for instance, in such problems as under-developed areas, world population growth and food production, and attention was directed to the few wide open spaces still relatively untenanted. Amazônia was an obvious example and Brazilian governments began to feel the need for a change of policy towards the region. The three services in Brazil took their responsibilities in the backlands seriously, the army supporting isolated populations through its frontier-detachments, the air force and navy transporting people and

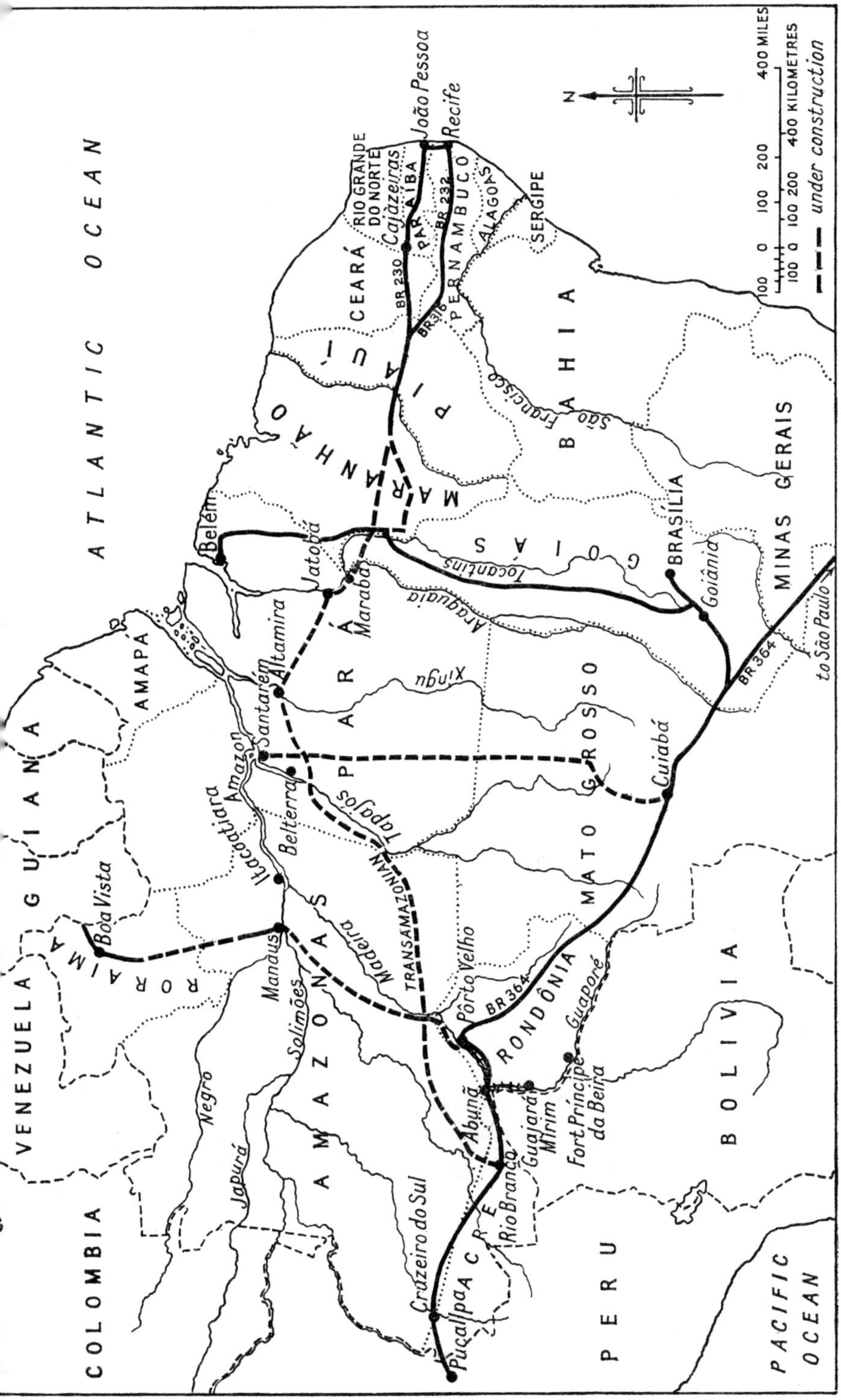

4 A network of roads will hasten the penetration of Amazônia

supplies and maintaining communications over the great distances prevailing in the region.

The military were therefore ready from 1964 to put the spotlight on Amazônia. Government leaders spoke of the need to integrate Amazônia with the rest of the country and to occupy the region effectively. During a visit to Manaus in 1968, President Costa e Silva warned that Brazil must either occupy Amazônia, or run the risk of losing it; General Albuquerque Lima, the Minister for regional development, spoke of a world struggle for control of raw materials and living-space, declaring that Brazil's inertia in developing Amazônia's resources was exposing the region to 'international covetousness'. The military commander in Belém, General Rodrigo Otávio Jordão was more explicit: Brazil must effectively occupy Amazônia, so that by the year 2000, when world population might reach from 6,000 to 6,500 million, Brazil could show not empty spaces but occupied land, thus avoiding the limitation of its sovereignty by alien impositions made in the name of the survival of Asian and African population surpluses.

Occupation, however, was primarily a matter of investment. Brazil was a country with scarce resources, and in the taking of decisions to use some of them in developing Amazônia, the question arose: would there be an adequate return for the nation on the money invested? Previous experience in the region suggested that caution should be exercised.

Ford versus Amazônia

There were various examples of how money could be lost in Amazonian ventures, but the classic was Henry Ford's attempt to re-establish large-scale rubber production. Ford was anxious to secure his own supplies and, it was suggested, to end his dependence on the British Empire, which controlled the world rubber trade through the Asian plantations that had virtually driven the wild rubber of Brazil from world markets.

He began in the late 1920s with typical determination, in a large area on the River Tapajós some distance from Santarém. The site was named Fordlândia and Ford, attending to the welfare of his workers, saw to it that the site had all the modern conveniences: a well-equipped hospital, homes, schools, ice-plants, clubs, recreation facilities, all the paraphernalia of a big, modern industrial enterprise.

After careful preparations and with the current resources of science at his disposal, Ford began to grow plantation rubber, using seeds from the region, and planting them in orderly rows. His first experiments were a failure: the young trees fell to a leaf fungus that spread rapidly through the plantations, as it had been unable to spread in the forest where the rubber trees grew far apart, protected by other trees and the vegetation.

Ford however refused to admit defeat. He brought in new seeds from the Far East, taken from improved, disease-resisting descendants of those that Wickham had obtained from Brazil, and moved to a new area where conditions promised to be more favourable. Here for a time things went better for the venture. The Second World War broke out and the pressure was on to increase rubber supplies to the Allied powers; an army of 18,000 workers was recruited on the coast to tap the wild rubber trees of the Amazonian jungle. The prospects for Ford now seemed excellent but he was still running into problems. A fanatical believer in paying high wages, he paid his labourers, scarce in a region where population was rarefied, daily rates that only encouraged them to work for a while, down tools and go back home to spend their savings or retire. Labour agitators added to the difficulties.

The war ended, with a large synthetic-rubber industry now established in the U.S.A. and Asian rubber supplies once more available. Ford had had enough of his Brazilian venture. Some twenty years and 15 million dollars after he had started, he admitted defeat, selling out to the Brazilian government for a mere 250,000 dollars. It was a sobering lesson for those who thought that the problems of the Amazon could be mastered by money and technology.

Despite the Ford withdrawal from Amazônia, the Brazilian authorities kept a wary eye on U.S. interest in the region and from 1964 there were indications that they feared a further upsurge of American activity. Private American companies, through local subsidiaries, came to hold concessions to sizeable areas in the state of Pará, and there was a hostile Brazilian reaction to a project put forward by an American body, the Hudson Institute, to establish in the region a 'Great Lakes' type system of inland navigation and to build a huge hydro-electric plant to supply cheap power; the scheme proposed for Brazil was part of a huge international plan to connect the river systems of seven countries and integrate transport in South America. It was likely that, quite apart from the scheme's technical interest, Brazilian policy-makers saw it as a potential 'thin end of the wedge' of American penetration into Amazônia. The Brazilians, meanwhile, cleaned the dust off their own plans to link the Amazon to the River Plate basin in Argentina, plans that included the big Lago da Paz (Peace Lake) project in northern Mato Grosso.

Development programmes for Amazônia

A vast, empty region of tropical forests and grasslands cut by the world's greatest river system, Amazônia accounts for 42 per cent of Brazil's total area, and comprises the two huge states of Pará (nearly four times larger than Italy) and Amazonas (three times the size of France), the state of Acre, and three federal territories, Rondônia, Roraima and Amapá. It is Brazil's most thinly populated region, with 3.2 million people scattered in settlements along the rivers but with nearly a million of them living in the municipal areas of the two largest cities, Belém and Manaus. Possessing a hot, damp climate, Amazônia has been described as ideal for insects, plants, reptiles and animals, but not for men.

For their livelihood, the Amazonenses depend on the traditional raw materials, such as jute and pepper (both introduced by the diligent Japanese), Brazil nuts, natural rubber, timber, and hides and skins. Private investment in industry has remained at a low level, and factories are concentrated around Belém and Manaus, which are the focal points of the region's development. The establishment of industries has, until recently, been slow because of the shortage of skilled labour, the limited availability of local capital and the long distances from Amazônia to markets in the more developed countries.

The implementation of a 'new deal' for Amazônia by the three administrations that followed the 1964 military coup, took advantage of experience gained elsewhere in Brazil. The new regional development agency, the Sudam, modelled on that already existing in the North-East, took the place of the old SPVEA[1] and was set up in 1966, with headquarters in Belém and jurisdiction over the whole 'legal area' of Amazônia (an administrative arrangement that added to Amazônia parts of Mato Grosso, Maranhão and Goiás). Sudam administered an

[1] Superintendency for the Economic Valorization of Amazônia.

elaborate system of incentives and tax concessions for firms ready to invest in development and set in motion a large number of agricultural and industrial projects, many of them in cattle-ranching in Pará and Mato Grosso.

Manaus, the capital of Western Amazônia, hardly seemed credible after the extraordinary period that ended with the collapse of the rubber boom. The fortunes made and lost at the gaming-tables, the imposing opera house presenting the world's finest singers, the lavish bordellos, the pretentious mansions built by the 'rubber barons', did not suggest that Manaus could ever settle down to life as a quiet, forgotten river-port isolated from the rest of Brazil. The town stagnated after its brief period of glory. Today, however, despite the decaying look of its faded wooden houses and of its shacks at the river's edge, Manaus has compensations—a small-town friendliness and a more personal style of life in keeping with its outpost status. The local people, forming a more closely-knit community, may even commiserate with the visitor when they hear he is from São Paulo. There is poverty but nobody need starve—there are plenty of big fish in the river; for the visitor there is a feeling of being closer to nature and of being far away from anywhere.

Manaus remains an outpost. By road one can go no further than Itacoatiara, about 180 miles down the river. For those who can afford it, there is the aeroplane, but from the vantage-point of Manaus it is clear that the objective of opening up the Amazônian interior will face considerable barriers. In November 1968 a ten-member expedition led by Father Calleri left Manaus to pacify the Atroari Indians in a region to be crossed by a federal road linking Manaus to Boa Vista and, ultimately, the Venezuelan border. Their massacre by the Atroaris 150 miles north of Manaus was one example of the difficulties that would have to be faced.

Because of this remoteness—Manaus is nearly two hours by jet from Belém—it was given special treatment by the federal government. The establishment of the Manaus free trade zone in 1967 was designed to improve living conditions and boost business activity by the elimination of import duties and excise taxes on foreign and national goods entering the zone. It was a first move in the process of integrating the region with the rest of Brazil. In the longer term, the concessions granted in the zone, together with the investment incentives offered by Sudam, were also intended to foster the growth of industry in Manaus, where a new industrial district was to accommodate a number of factories.

The free trade zone offered a golden opportunity to make a 'fast buck'. They swarmed in from Panama, speaking Spanish and looking like Arabs, or from Brooklyn and the Bronx, with their white cloth caps and American accents filling the Hotel Amazonas and the Lord Hotel. The Douglas DC3s flew the Japanese-made goods in from Panama, to fill the counters of the little shops, whose new tenants sold to the holiday tourist trade and tried to bribe the Air Force to ship surplus goods south.

In the midst of all this hectic trading, first scorned and later absorbed and controlled by the established Manaus merchants, it came as a surprise to find a British-style supermarket in operation. The largest supplier of foodstuffs to the city, the 'Produtos Finos' supermarket was an Anglo-Brazilian venture, by Booth Brazil Limited (Booth Lines had been operating in the region for over 100 years) and the Amazonas Development Company, headed by Isaac Sabbá, the region's elder statesman, who since his arrival in Manaus as a boy in the 1920s had set an example of what hard work and vision could achieve in Amazônia. On the supermarket's shelves were Lyons, Cadbury's and Chivers, side by side with the staple Brazilian foods. The Manaus housewives, if they did not take readily to steak and kidney pudding and took time to understand how to eat corn flakes, appreciated the quality.

It was all part of a new deal for the region, with political and psychological effects. In both the federal and state governments there was apparent determination to develop the resources of Amazônia and the population of the region seemed to be convinced that the policy of isolation had ended.

The danger to the Indians

For one element in the Amazonian population these were highly unfavourable developments.

Scattered among the land of Amazônia and the Centre-West were the greater part of Brazil's Indian populations, for which there was a large reserve area in northern Mato Grosso, the national park of the Xingu. There the brothers Vilas-Boas in the tradition established by the soldier-explorer, Marshal Rondon, carried on the work of endeavouring to protect the Indians against the worst effects of the inroads of 'civilization'.

From the time when the Portuguese colonization and the instinct of self-preservation drove the tribes inland to where they could escape from the white man's depredations, they had been fighting their own hazardous battle for survival, decimated by the white man's diseases, and harried by the armed prospectors, rubber-tappers and cattle farmers pushing Brazil's economic frontier further into the interior.[1]

Unofficial estimates were that they now numbered 100,000. They were seriously threatened by the impact of a way of life completely alien to their own traditions. Their fate had been much better than those of the Indian populations in the U.S.A. and Argentina, or even in the other countries of South America, but the prospects for their survival as an independent culture looked bad, as Amazônia and the Centre-West were increasingly penetrated by the long-distance trunk-roads and telecommunications networks that would increase the diffusion of modern Brazilian culture throughout the regions.

The move on Western Amazônia

In the drive to occupy and integrate Amazônia with the Centre-South, the right arm of the pincer movement was the Belém-Brasília' and the left the BR-364, the trunk road reaching out from the state of São Paulo to Peru.

For this turning of the western flank of Amazônia, the Centre-West—the states of Goiás and Mato Grosso— was the platform or spring-board from which the opening up of the far western territories was being organized. In this movement, Brazilians from the South and the North-East and the big cattle ranches backed by São Paulo capital, were playing a prominent part, but the spearhead was military.

Thus, in western Mato Grosso, the territory of Rondônia and the state of Acre, areas long neglected by the federal government, army engineers were building an 1,800 mile highway linking these isolated lands to the principal population centres of Brazil, to Brasília, but more important, to São Paulo and the other industrial and business centres. When the road reached the Peruvian border opposite Pucallpa, it would be one of the arteries of the slow process of Latin American integration; with the

[1] Colonel Fawcett, the vanished explorer who travelled widely in the South American interior, also wrote of this aspect in his *Exploration Fawcett,* London, Hutchinson, 1953.

Peruvians having completed their share of the road-building, the adventurous would be able to drive from Rio to Lima across the heart of South America.

In September 1969[1] the Fifth Construction Engineering Battalion, with headquarters at Pôrto Velho in Rondônia, had just brought the all-weather dirt road beginning at Cuiabá, capital of Mato Grosso, to Abunã, a village some 130 miles on from Pôrto Velho. The road was being pushed on into Acre and the target was to reach the Peruvian border with a 'pioneer road'.

Meanwhile, the Battalion, some 1,000 sappers and 700 attached civilians, many of whom came from the primitive life of hunting or tapping rubber-trees in the jungle, also had the task of consolidating and maintaining the road throughout its length; permanent concrete bridges had to be built for the innumerable river crossings, many of which were negotiated by wooden bridges or ferries. An increasing volume of traffic between Cuiabá and Pôrto Velho made this work all the more necessary, and it was liable to be interrupted or hindered by the heavy tropical rains falling between October and May. In the rainy season, however, there was no lack of tasks for the sappers' skills, which were welcome in the region. Pôrto Velho had benefited from them, in the form of a new, asphalted main-street, improved water supply and some low-cost housing. Local tradespeople appreciated the increase in custom brought by the military and began to see improved prospects for the region; the town's taxi-drivers bought new cars from São Paulo. The civil engineers in Cuiabá found a big new operation with work that could be sub-contracted to them.

The officers and warrant officers of the Fifth, under the command of Colonel Carlos Weber, a Gaúcho, had volunteered for this assignment. Among the officers and men the various regions of Brazil were broadly represented; of the other ranks, some had been sent to Amazônia as a punishment, but the local Amazonense element in the Battalion was growing, with the unit recruiting twice a year from towns in the region. The operation enjoyed the logistical support available to a military operation (although two civilian construction firms also worked with the Battalion on portions of the road). The Air Force in support of the Battalion, had moved more than 3,000 tons of cargo and

[1] The date of the author's visit to the Battalion.

2,000 passengers from various points in Brazil, with C-130, C-54 and C-47 aircraft. Other materials had been brought by river, by other army units in the region. Colonel Weber strove to apply the methods of private enterprise to the operation.

The difficulties of maintaining morale and discipline among detachments spaced out along the road and living under oppressive conditions, the problems involved in breaking through the dense tropical forest and in building roads and bridges to stand up to the rigours of the dry season and the impact of the rainstorms, were examples of what the Battalion faced. Far worse, however, than the monotony of life and the loneliness, was the problem of malaria in the region, which at times inflicted serious casualties, despite the medical efforts made. There were few people in the backlands of Rondônia who managed to escape this disease. Under these conditions, Colonel Weber, who liked to quote Churchill to British visitors, had taken care to create an 'ideology' for the operation and to convince officers and men of its value, for the development of the region and within the broader, national context.

Abunã, where one of the engineering companies held a barbecue to celebrate the completion of that stage of the road, was a hundred or so houses by the side of the River Madeira, with Bolivia across the water. It had a large, ramshackle hotel built by 'the English' during the rubber boom, but several thousand miles removed from Trust House standards. It was also one of the thriving centres of insect life in the region. The 'pium', the buffalo gnat, attacked the pale-faced visitor in swarms, and covered its victim with weals, leaving a minute drop of blood in the centre of each. It was said to be only thwarted by a good layer of Vick Vapo-Rub, which would entangle its legs and wings and, one would hope, asphyxiate it; this, however, one only found out weeks after the event!

The pium was in any case the least of the troubles around Abunã. A corporal from Pernambuco at the barbecue had had 14 attacks of malaria, and a writer told of two sappers, with 16 and 17 bouts of the disease behind them, taking a 200 cruzeiro bet as to who would have had the most by Christmas.[1] It was in this area that the builders of the railway during the rubber boom lost hundreds of lives and spent two years in crossing 30 miles of swamp land; the Fifth Battalion, working round the clock, took

[1] Walder de Góis, *A Marcha além do Oeste,* Goiânia, 1969, p. 130.

40 days. The jungle gets its own back on those who violate it and the graves in the battalion's cemetery in Pôrto Velho mark the casualties suffered. They include Colonel Weber's son, who died in an accident; eight sappers and 18 civilians died in the course of the operations.

It fell to the Fifth Battalion, in particular to Lieutenant-Colonel Oliveira, to administer and wind up the affairs of the legendary Madeira-Mamoré railway, running from Pôrto Velho to Guajará Mirim on the Bolivian border. Its construction began early in the 1870s, after the Bolivians, anxious to obtain an Atlantic outlet for their trade, had negotiated the building of a railway through to Pôrto Velho, which could not be reached by river because of the numerous rapids on the River Madeira. From the town, ships could sail to Manaus and Belém, and thence to foreign markets.

An American firm was contracted and capital was supplied by the London market; it was the beginning of a disastrous venture.

In the face of great natural difficulties, of malaria, yellow fever, and attacks by the local Indian tribes, first one contractor and then another abandoned the project after laying only five miles of track and surveying only a fraction of the 230 miles that the railway was to cover.[1]

Time went by and the rubber boom came to revive the interest of Bolivia in winning markets for its high-grade rubber. In 1903 it signed a treaty ceding the territory of Acre to Brazil, which undertook to build the railway, and also called on the services of American contractors, who began work in 1907. The line took five years to build, being completed just before the collapse of the boom, and casualties were such that the laying of every sleeper was said to have cost a man's life. Workers from Europe, the Americas and the Caribbean took part in this disastrous epic. In the railway's workshops in Pôrto Velho the author met descendants of West Indians who had worked in the construction gangs.

The Madeira-Mamoré railway lived on. It was for long a financial millstone round the neck of the Brazilian government, which at last decided to eradicate it. The Fifth Battalion built a 230-mile road from Pôrto Velho to Guajará Mirim to replace it, and this legacy from Rondônia's past slipped back into history.

[1] Willard Price, *The Amazing Amazon*, London, Heinemann, 1953, pp. 139-43.

The army on the frontier

The three services find in Amazônia the tasks that give them a sense of mission. This is apparent in the idea of 'military colonies' and is seen in the army's frontier detachments, which are spaced out along the border with Brazil's neighbours in Bolivia, Peru, Colombia and Venezuela. These units show the flag, cultivate the feeling of nationality among the frontier populations and act in support of their welfare, the soldier sometimes becoming in the process farmer, small businessman, road-builder, teacher, doctor or dentist.

Some aspects of this supporting function could be seen at Fort Príncipe da Beira in Rondônia, where a ruined but impressive fort of red stone marked a point chosen by the Portuguese in colonial times to check Spanish incursions from across the River Guaporé. In bucolic surroundings, a frontier platoon busied itself with laying down an infrastructure for settlement of the area: a small school, a brickworks, carpentry shop and other facilities to help the local people engage in small farming.

It was surprising to find a strong, competitive spirit amongst these frontier units. 'We are the best on the frontier' ('Somos os melhores da fronteira') was the slogan on the front wall of the barracks of the frontier company at Guajará-Mirim on the Bolivian border, a little town of 6,000 people.

The company had an addiction to spit and polish that the author had rarely seen elsewhere in Brazil. The spirit of mañana (in Brazil amanhã) that Europeans expect to find all over South America had been banished. A slogan painted on the water-tower read 'Don't wait, do it' and the company, it seemed, was there to prod the local community into development-mindedness. The unit had organized a small 'zoo' from the local fauna, to add to the town's points of interest; the animals, the brightly-coloured parrots and even the boa constrictor neatly coiled up in its pit, all looked clean and shining.

The heat at Guajará was also remarkable. It always pays on such occasions to travel with a quarter-master, like Major Corrêa of the Fifth Battalion, a North-easterner from Piauí who was the author's guide; when the heat was at its worst, he had the ability to conjure up unlimited quantities of chilled beer.

A return for investment?

The compensation for the sacrifices and expenses incurred in building roads like the BR-364 lay initially in the change and progress brought to the forgotten Brazilians of this remote region, in bringing hope and in introducing concrete improvements to the shabby towns and villages of an impoverished, sparsely populated region.

Of considerable importance, however, was the possibility of the pay-off for the large investment made, through the stimulus given to local production. There was always a hope that the new roads would assist the handling and transport of new sources of wealth and in the case of Rondônia it could be that one development would ultimately make a large contribution to the costs.

A boom in the mining of cassiterite, or tin ore, shook Rondônia out of its stagnation, making it Brazil's principal tin producing area. Here the old and the new clashed. Prospectors and mining companies vied for supremacy in the mining areas and bloodshed was on occasions narrowly averted, in the struggle between modern industrial and commercial methods and the individualistic, old-fashioned processes of the 'tin-panners'. A local expert, with international experience of the tin business, saw the area as having the potential of another Malaysia and as offering good prospects for the other minerals usually associated with cassiterite. A further big discovery was reported on the border of the state of Amazonas with Mato Grosso. It was expected that a feeder road would be completed to Alto Candeias, the main producing area; the cassiterite was at present flown out to the main highway, and from there went by road to the smelters in the Centre-South.

These developments raised expectations of a better deal for a region that badly needed it. The penetration of a region equipped with a resistant, aggressive nature was going ahead. Civilian construction firms were working to link Manaus by road to the BR-364 at Pôrto Velho and when this was ready, Manaus would have for the first time a land communication with the industrial and business areas of São Paulo and the Centre-South—a landmark in the history of Amazônia. In the broader, Inter-American sense, when the Peruvian and Brazilian portions of the larger highways were finished, the Atlantic economy would be joined to the economy of the Pacific.

10 Brazil and the Year 2000

Three exponents of development

It was in 1930 that the national struggle for development began in earnest, pursuing its uneven course in the following decades, which included periods of stability but also crises of varying degrees of severity. In the 40 years that brought Brazil to the decade of the 1970s, three men made their particular contributions to the history of the times and to the process of development.

The first, Getúlio Vargas, left his mark on an era when the country underwent rapid economic and social change and Brazilians began to develop a stronger national consciousness. Vargas' assumption of power led to a renewal of the top layers of the ruling classes and he carried out some partial reforms of political life, enlarging the franchise and improving the electoral procedure. He worked for greater political unity, curbed the power of the states, particularly of São Paulo, and brought them increasingly under the control of the central government. He had a sense of mission, hoping to create a new mentality among Brazilians and to increase the participation of the masses, to which he appealed directly, in the political life of the country.

His record in advancing political development was, however, controversial, as his actions often seemed to be motivated by his intention to keep himself in power. His dominance of the stage for so many years hindered the emergence and training of new leaders and left the country ill-prepared for the political crises of the future.

During his long rule, Brazil moved away from dependence on a colonial-type agriculture catering to foreign markets, and turned to industrialization. Vargas stimulated the growth of national enterprise but also called on foreign capital when he felt that this was in the national interest. He furthered the process of generating growth within the country. In industry, his paternalism expressed itself in social legislation designed principally to benefit the urban workers and in the forms of labour organization that he determined for them. In the economic field Vargas substantially used his monopoly of power to bring

Brazil out of backwardness into a more modern environment, dragging a part of Brazil from the nineteenth into the twentieth century.

Juscelino Kubitschek based his appeal to Brazilians on nationalism and development, issues that Vargas had publicized; in his early career he grew up in the Vargas political tradition, but later rapidly became a leader in his own right. A conservative politician, he displayed a virtuoso ability to use to the full the resources of the political system, but he did little or nothing to cure its defects. His attractive personality made him one of the most popular of Brazilian Presidents: his optimism, belief in the future of the country and political tolerance were among the qualities, typical of Brazilians, that found a ready acceptance among them.

Kubitschek enhanced the nationalism of his fellow-countrymen and awakened them to the challenge of developing Brazil's latent resources, stimulating their self-confidence and directing their attention towards the interior. Thus, he took a historic step in moving the federal capital inland, and in his policy towards the North-East showed his interest in fostering development in the poorer regions and making them more fully part of Brazil. In advocating a Pan-American development project, later embodied in the Alliance for Progress, he looked outside the boundaries of his own country to the needs of Latin America.

Under Kubitschek, Brazil greatly expanded its industrial capacity and despite a certain neglect of other sectors, advanced more rapidly towards the goal of becoming a modern, industrial nation. Unfortunately, however, he was prodigal in his methods, and his gifts of enterprise and imagination outran the country's ability to pay, creating serious problems for his successors. The boom of the Kubitschek term of office carried within it the seeds of the future crisis.

The third leader, Castello Branco, was that familiar personage in Latin American history—the inheritor of disaster, brought to power at a time when growing disorder had pushed the country to the brink of collapse. In driving back the forces of chaos and organizing recovery, Castello taught the distasteful lesson that Brazil must try to live according to its means. Austere and totally different in personality from Vargas and Kubitschek, he undertook a task of guaranteed unpopularity and brought to it the soldierly virtues. He himself did not seek popular esteem, nor did he receive it: apart from those who worked with him, his compatriots were slow to appreciate the positive contribution made by this singular figure and by his administration.

The three-year term of office of Castello was characterized by an intensive effort to reform and modernize institutions and attitudes in various sectors of the national life. Politically speaking, Castello was unsuccessful in fulfilling the targets of reconstruction that he set himself, achievement of which was frustrated by the circumstances and pressures, including military ones, prevailing after 1964. In other respects, however, in administration, in economic and financial stewardship, his government showed considerable capacity for innovation and was highly creative, laying a foundation on which succeeding governments were able to build. It was successful in making a sharp and salutary change of course that later opened new perspectives for the country's economic development.

At the beginning of the decade of the 1970s, it was clear that in one respect Brazil had changed considerably: since 1964 there had been a near-revolution in administration, in the introduction of more effective government. With this went a coherent economic policy that gave the green light to private enterprise, to businessmen and industrialists, particularly to the exporters. Likewise, the state governments and municipal administrations were under pressure to endorse and put into practice the new development ethic. In this whole process, considerable responsibility was vested in the technocrats, men largely without political affiliations.

From the achievement of substantial economic progress from 1967 onwards, one deduction seemed inescapable: the by-passing of the old, traditional political classes, who were removed from playing any significant part in economic policy-making and execution, had greatly benefited progress.

Nevertheless, the armed forces, which as one of the few organized institutions in Brazil undertook the organization of the country's development in 1964, had also assumed responsibility for its political aspect. The disturbing feature was that, as the country recovered and advanced economically, the political system closed: government with authority, as exemplified by Castello Branco, later lapsed into authoritarianism and repression, pushed in this direction by the activities of the revolutionary Left. The danger was that unless well-directed, positive steps were taken to open the political system and to train the political leaders of the future, Brazil would once more find herself in the position in which Vargas had left it: without a civilian elite organized and ready to govern.

Brazil and the crystal-gazers

Few countries are less predictable than Brazil, but this did not prevent the outbreak of an epidemic of futurology in the late '60s.

It was all very depressing for Brazilians, who, like everybody else, resent pessimistic forecasts by foreigners. Herman Kahn and Anthony Wiener of the Hudson Institute, the well-known 'think-tank' at Croton-on-Hudson outside New York, were taking a particularly bearish view of the prospects for Brazil, traditionally 'the country of the future'. Their book *The Year 2000* was published in 1967—a difficult time for Brazilians, who for three years had been suffering the rigours of belt-tightening and disinflation, and were in no mood for predictions that Brazil, then admittedly a poor country, would still be one at the end of the century.[1]

The authors made clear the nature and scope of their world-wide study. According to the Preface, it was 'a framework for speculation' and a 'far from an exhaustive set of conjectures about every important element of the future'; still less was it 'an attempt to predict any particular aspect of the future'.[2] In their opening chapter, 'Change and continuity', the authors made their 'most important caveat': that 'almost any day has some chance of bringing up some new crisis or unexpected event that becomes a historical turning-point, diverting current tendencies so that expectations for the distant future must shift. Over any period of decades, at least one such shift, and probably several, are likely—and the turning-point may come at any moment'.[3] The speculative character of the exercise was therefore unmistakable. Within its framework however, the division of the world's countries into groups, in accordance with their degrees of development, was a natural target for controversy when a country looked at its ranking in the league table.

Kahn and Wiener, considering where the nations might stand in the year 2000, on the basis of levels of income and industrial development, adopted a division into five classes: pre-industrial,

[1] Average annual income per head in all Brazil is currently around 450 dollars, but there are great variations in the various regions.
[2] H. Kahn and A. J. Wiener, *The Year 2000,* Preface, p. xix.
[3] Ibid, p. 13.

partially industrialized or transitional, industrial, mass consumption or advanced industrial, and finally, at the top, post-industrial. To each class they assigned broad ranges of annual income per head; thus at the affluent top was a range of something over 4,000 to perhaps 20,000 dollars per head, and at the bottom a wretched 50 to 200 dollars.[1]

The authors also drew up a table of 'rather impressionistic, but not wholly unreasonable economic ranking', including forecast levels of population and corresponding broadly to the five classes.[2] The highest ranking, which the authors broke down into 'visibly post-industrial' and 'early post-industrial', embraced the U.S.A., Japan, Canada, the Scandinavian countries, Switzerland, France, W. Germany and the Benelux countries in the first sub-group, while the U.K., the Soviet Union, Italy and six others were placed in the second. The worst-off-to-be included parts of Africa, the Arab world, Asia and Latin America, where the gap in living standards, in comparison with the wealthy countries, would have 'widened abysmally'.

The authors expected a few large, partially industrialized countries to account for half of an estimated world population of 6,400 million. These nations, in which annual income per head would be between 200 to 600 dollars, would include Brazil, Pakistan, China, India, Indonesia, the United Arab Republic and Nigeria. Of the Latin American countries, only Argentina and Venezuela would join the ranks of the 'mass consumption' second group, while Mexico, Uruguay, Chile, Cuba, Colombia, Peru and Panama would be among the 'mature industrial' countries of the third. Brazil, in the fourth, was therefore placed well behind many of its neighbours in Latin America.

Kahn and Wiener also presented some 'surprise-free' economic projections, described as ones that seemed less surprising than any other specific possibilities. These were worked out after projecting a number of variables such as population, literacy, gross national product, energy sources and military strength. Among the ten major countries considered, the U.S.A., the Soviet Union and Japan were to be economic super-powers at the end of the century. Among 19 contender countries, Brazil was seen as probably moving from an annual income per head of 280 dollars in 1965 to just over 500 dollars in the year 2000, and as needing 130 years to reach the current level of gross national product

[1] Ibid, p. 58. [2] Ibid, p. 60.

per head of the U.S.A. (Sweden would take only 11 years, the United Kingdom 19, Japan 22 and India 117).[1]

Much depended on the figures used in the calculations. The forecasts were expressed in two main variables, the rate of population growth and the growth rate of the GNP. Thus, for Brazil it was supposed that population would grow at 3.1 per cent up to 1975, 2.9 from then to 1985 and 2.4 per cent in the last 15 years of the century. Three rates were taken as possible annual average rates of economic growth during the period, a low rate of 3 per cent, a medium rate of 4.5 and a high rate of 7 per cent. The medium rate had been used to forecast that in the year 2000 the average Brazilian, in terms of GNP per head, would be earning only a meagre 500 dollars a year.

It was a grim prospect for Brazilians and their governments; a leading weekly, in an illustration of what his predictions implied for the future, named Herman Kahn 'a horseman of the Apocalypse'. When he visited Brazil towards the end of 1969, many were anxious to change his mind and his figures. These had taken 1965, an unfavourable time, as a base-year and since then things had started to move. Brazil had begun to record some much improved growth rates, after the period of sacrifice endured during the Castello Branco administration.

The futurologist proved ready to think again about Brazil when he had taken a closer look at the country. The impression was gained, however, that he was unconvinced by Brazil's ambitions for major power status later in the century. Speaking to businessmen and industrialists in São Paulo, he impressed upon them what was being achieved in Japan, quoting a rousing ditty exalting teamwork and sung by the workers of the Matsushita Electric Company—a typical example of Japanese awareness of the effort required for rapid development.

The suspicions of Brazilians that Herman Kahn did not take their country's prospects too seriously were awakened by a rumour circulating in São Paulo that when taken out in a helicopter by the state governor, Abreu Sodré, to see the impressive expansion of São Paulo, he had to be frequently prompted, to get him to take note of all the large, modern factories. On a further visit in 1970, however, he relented enough to allow that Brazilians might after all enjoy a better deal and reach a per capita income of 1,200 dollars in the year 2000. It was hardly the place in the sun to which Brazilians aspired.

[1] Ibid, p. 149

The book of Kahn and Wiener opened up the debate on the country's future, as Brazilians took up the challenge of showing rationally that Brazil must do better than the dire forecasts of the futurologists indicated. The contributors to this debate included Reis Velloso, the Planning Minister, Roberto Campos, then President of an investment bank, and Mário Henrique Simonsen, whose book *Brasil 2001* identified the principal problems to be tackled over the next three decades.

Simonsen was head of the post-graduate school of economics at the principal research centre, the Getúlio Vargas Foundation in Rio, director of a leading investment bank and a spokesman for the technocracy. He identified five sectors in which efforts should be concentrated, if Brazil was to break out of the vicious circle of poverty: savings and investment, education and technology, population growth, trade and policy-making.

Like Kahn and Wiener, Simonsen was impressed by the Japanese example of high growth rates achieved by a remarkable national effort in savings, expressed in a rate of investment equivalent to 35 per cent of the gross domestic product, more than double the current Brazilian rate. He warned Brazilians against euphoria over the high growth rates—8 to 9 per cent—of 1968/70; Brazil was not accustomed to the sacrifices required to keep on growing rapidly, nor to the political austerity or the rigorous attitude to government spending that would be indispensable in the future.[1] These unaccustomed virtues would moreover have to be complemented by a positive attitude to business profits and their reinvestment, to individual saving through the stock-market and to a continued flow of foreign capital.

Simonsen preached the need for Brazil to reverse its previous neglect of education and to demonstrate this change of attitude in government, where the Education Ministry had traditionally been a second-class ministry, usually filled after a process of bargaining among the politicians. Analysing the post-war reconstruction and advance of Japan and W. Germany, and the slow progress recorded in the world's under-developed areas, he argued for full recognition of the part to be played by education and technology, concluding that Brazil's progress over the next 30 years would in good degree depend on its investment in its own citizens. In the past, education in Brazil had provided a shining example of how it was possible, by stupidity, to wipe out the productivity of an entire sector.

[1] The growth rate for 1971 was over 11 per cent.

In his analysis of the educational system, Simonsen found many grounds for criticism, in the high levels of absenteeism, in the high costs per pupil contrasting with low pay for teachers, and finally in the divorce from the requirements of the labour and careers market. Technical education was also regarded as being in the second class. It was all part of the wastage of the latent potential of Brazil's human resources. Writing a year after the publication of *Brasil 2001,* however, Simonsen gave a more optimistic picture of the current approach to education, in terms of governmental attitudes, of funds invested and policies. There appeared to be grounds for hope that the decade of the '70s might see the educational revolution that Brazil so desperately needed.

Simonsen also took aim against the 'arithmetic of the rabbits'.[1] Population in Brazil had increased ninefold in the last 100 years, a remarkable increase, even if rapid growth had been a world-wide phenomenon. Brazilians had obeyed to the full the biblical commandment to grow and multiply, more completely even than other peoples in Latin America, which held the world record.

As a mathematician, for whom the denominator in calculating income per head was Brazil's teeming population, Simonsen rejected the traditional acceptance of, and pride in, a fast-growing population as a presumed means of enhancing the country's status, enlarging its market, helping to occupy its empty spaces and securing its borders against intruders. The case of Brazil was exceptional Simonsen argued. It was facing an unprecedented population explosion, which could only be desirable for a government whose main anxiety was not to increase its people's living standards, but to swell the ranks of its infantry. The explosive nature of the growth swept away the arguments of those who said that development and greater prosperity would easily absorb an expanding population.

The difficulty that Brazilians had in agreeing on this issue was apparent to the foreign visitor. There was resistance to birth control, even when dressed up as family-planning, and opposition from the Catholic Church, which could not bring itself to approve 'the pill'. The need for action to moderate population growth was most pressing in the North-East. President Médici himself, when he visited the region during the drought of

[1] *Brasil 2001,* p. 99.

1970, was struck by the large families that the poorest peasants struggled to maintain. People were, however, slow to revise their thinking. There were too many who, perhaps unconsciously, were helping to push Brazil towards an Indian-type poverty rather than a European-type prosperity, towards th… dards of Pernambuco rather than those of São P

The challenges of the future

The evidence shows that the tempo of change for Brazil in the coming three decades will be rapid, as it struggles to recover lost time and narrow the wide gap between its living standards and those of the developed countries of the West.

Although the most recent information points to some slackening of the rate of population growth during this period, it is probably reasonable to forecast that in 1980 Brazil's population will exceed 120 million and in the year 2000, 210 million.[1] The experts confirm that the exodus from the countryside and the resulting urban explosion will continue. In 1980, they calculate, 80m Brazilians will live in the towns and cities and 40m. in the countryside; the situation of 1940, when two lived in the rural areas foı every one in the cities, will thus have been completely reversed by 1980. Then, for example, the state of São Paulo will number nearly 24m. inhabitants, of which 21m. will be in the urban areas.

Nationally, growth will be most rapid in cities currently with over 500,000 people, which nearly double every ten years; jobs available in them will have to increase in step with an expanding labour force. Eight million homes will have to be built in the decade of the '70s to cope with the need for new houses, the replacement of old ones and the requirements of slum clearance. Massive investment will have to be made to provide building-materials, water and power supplies, drainage, schools and medical facilities. Brazilian farms will have to raise their output to meet the growing food needs of the cities, producing at prices accessible to the urban masses and relying increasingly on mechanization.

Looking ahead to the year 2000, a Brazilian expert sees Greater São Paulo and Greater Rio as holding 19m. and 15m. respectively, with industries expanding in their metropolitan

[1] These estimates are based on a 2.8 per cent growth rate.

areas and in the region between them.[1] Another writer suggests that these two cities and Belo Horizonte would then be 'integral units in one vast megalopolis stretching 1,000 miles along the Atlantic Coast and containing 100m. people, almost half the country's total population'. This area would 'encompass a large part of South America's industrial heartland and sap other areas of their human and capital resources, thus aggravating the already serious regional disparity'.[2]

Outside the cities of Brazil, however, other developments of national significance will be taking place. The federal road-building programmes of the National Transport Plan, as well as those of the states and municipalities, will speed the process of integration of the country and strengthen its links with its neighbours. The roads will bring new settlements and facilitate the discovery and development of natural resources, but equally they will help migrants to find their way to the overcrowded cities. They will accelerate change, for the roads have traditionally been the economic and social lifelines of Brazil. A similar part will be played by the telecommunications networks, bringing Brazilians in the distant regions into closer touch with the culture and the business and industrial life of the new Brazil; communications satellites may be used to advance educational programmes. These factors will further the process of more effective control and occupation of the national territory. The 'two Brazils' will move towards a greater unity.

The changes occurring at home are likely to be accompanied by some modification of Brazil's international relations.

In the early 1970s, as economic progress began to enhance Brazil's status, there were indications of the future political role that it might play. In South America, its central position in the land mass, where it bordered on many other countries, was likely to give it the opportunity to exercise a dominant influence in the region, where it might as a result expect less trouble-free relations with its neighbours than in the past.

Its assumption of a leading political role would hardly be to the liking of the Spanish-speaking countries of South America. This would also be the case economically. Brazilian industrialists and businessmen would seek to expand their sales in Latin

[1] H. Maksoud, in 'São Paulo in the year 2000', *Futures,* Vol. 1 number 3, Guildford, March 1969.

[2] Frances M. Foland, in 'Whither Brazil', *Inter-American Economic Affairs,* Winter 1970.

America. Above all, Brazil promised to become a centre for the international companies to supply the 11 member-countries of the Latin American Free Trade Association (Lafta). There were signs, in the pace-making motor-vehicle industry for instance, that the parent companies in the U.S.A. and W. Europe would raise the status of their Brazilian subsidiaries and transfer to them the task of supplying the Lafta market.

The last three decades would be a period of the sharing of world leadership by a few great powers—the U.S.A., the U.S.S.R., Japan and the enlarged European Economic Community among them. Detaching itself increasingly from American influence—the U.S.A. would remain a very important trading partner and Japan would become one—Brazil would strengthen her political, economic and cultural links with W. Europe, from where had come some of the principal elements in its population. In a minor key, it would maintain links with Africa, the spiritual home of part of its people.

Will Brazilians respond to the challenges of development offered to them?

Sceptical foreign observers, looking at the past record, may doubt the ability of Brazilians to make their country a leading world power by the year 2000. After all, they may say, if Brazil has been unable to provide satisfactory living-standards for the nearly 100 million of today, should one expect it to do so for over 200 million at the end of the century? Moreover, is it likely that a leading power will emerge from an environment where in many areas a hot, tropical climate discourages sustained effort?

By way of light-hearted argument that the Brazilian is ill-equipped to face the problems involved in transforming his country, critics may even point to that engaging, popular fiction, 'God is a Brazilian', as evidence of too much trust in the divine providence and of a certain lack of self-reliance.

Lacking the austere virtues necessary for lasting success, they argue, the Brazilians try to compensate with the gift of improvisation, typically displayed in the artistry of the great negro football players, in the reactions of the ordinary Brazilian to the unexpected need, mishap or breakdown, and in the ability to fix things that goes by the name of 'jeito'. The jeito, they say, is all too often the substitute for the unexciting but necessary qualities and activities. Thus, the routine of regular, preventive care and maintenance, the careful management of resources with a view to future needs, are alien to the temperament of many

Brazilians; they are not concerned about such things, confident that with good-humoured aplomb they can fix things 'in a jiffy'. This, the critics conclude, is not enough!

It would, however, be unjust to Brazilians to pass over their positive qualities: the patriotism and quickness of mind of the average citizen, for example, the factory worker's capacity for work and ability to learn, the powers of endurance of the peasant—all considerable national assets, given authentic leadership that is anxious to mobilize them and give them a stake in the country. If then there are Brazilian failings that arouse misgivings, there are qualities that inspire optimism. In face of the often unexploited resources and qualities of Brazil and the Brazilians it would be rash therefore summarily to write off their chances of success.

The next three decades will be years of rapid change. The pressure will be on Brazilians to modify their attitudes and opinions, as the process of making Brazil one country gathers pace. Self and family-oriented, relatively uninterested in the problems of the community, Brazilians are likely to become more involved in the lives of their less fortunate countrymen in regions coming progressively nearer. How Brazilians will respond to these challenges is a crucial question.

Whoever has travelled in Brazil and met the ordinary people, with their sometimes blind faith in their country's future, is bound to hope that in the years to come the great potential lying dormant in them will be increasingly realized.

Selected Bibliography

In English

Baklanoff, E. N. (ed.) *New Perspectives of Brazil,* Nashville, Tennessee, Vanderbilt University Press, 1966.

Baklanoff, E. N. (ed.) *The Shaping of Modern Brazil,* Baton Rouge, Louisiana State University, 1969.

Bates, H. W. *The Naturalist on the River Amazons,* London, Dent, 1969.

Bello, José Maria *A History of Modern Brazil 1889-1964,* Stanford, California, Stanford University Press, 1966.

Bourne, Richard *Political Leaders of Latin America,* Harmondsworth, Penguin, 1969.

Freyre, Gilberto *The Masters and the Slaves: a study in the development of Brazilian civilization,* London, Weidenfeld and Nicolson, 1956. Revised edition.

Furtado, Celso *Diagnosis of the Brazilian Crisis,* Berkeley and Los Angeles, University of California Press, 1965.

Hall, A. L. *Social and Economic Obstacles to Agrarian Reform in North-Eastern Brazil,* University of Glasgow, 1970.

Hirschman, Albert O. *Journeys towards Progress,* New York, Twentieth Century Fund, 1963.

Kahn, Herman and Wiener, Anthony J. *The year 2000: a framework for speculation on the next thirty-three years,* New York and London, Macmillan, 1967.

Lenard, Alexander *The Valley of the Latin Bear,* London, Gollancz, 1965.

Marshall, Andrew *Brazil,* London, Thames and Hudson, 1966.

Medina, José Toribio *The Discovery of the Amazon,* New York, American Geographical Society, 1934.

Millar, George *Orellana Discovers the Amazon,* London, Heinemann, 1954.

Moss, Robert *Urban Guerrillas,* London, Temple Smith, 1972.

Phelps, Gilbert *The Last Horizon,* London, Charles Knight, 1971. 2nd edition.

Rodrigues, José Honório *The Brazilians: their character and aspirations,* Austin, University of Texas Press, 1967.

Schneider, Ronald M. *The Political System of Brazil: emergence of a 'modernizing' authoritarian regime 1964-70,* New York and London, Columbia University Press, 1971.

St. Clair, David *The Mighty, Mighty Amazon,* London, Souvenir Press, 1968.

Skidmore, Thomas E. *Politics in Brazil 1930-64,* New York, Oxford University Press, 1967.

Smith, T. Lynn *Brazil: People and Institutions,* Baton Rouge, Louisiana State University, 1963. Revised edition.

Stepan, Alfred *The Military in Politics: changing patterns in Brazil,* New Jersey, Princeton University Press, 1971.

Veliz, Claudio (ed.) *Obstacles to Change in Latin America,* London, Oxford University Press for The Royal Institute of International Affairs, 1965.

Veliz, Claudio (ed.) *The politics of conformity in Latin America,* London, Oxford University Press for The Royal Institute of International Affairs, 1967.

Wagley, Charles *An Introduction to Brazil,* New York and London, Columbia University Press. Revised edition 1971.

Warriner, Doreen *Land Reform in Principle and Practice,* Oxford, Clarendon Press, 1969.

In Portuguese

Campos, Roberto de Oliveira *Do outro lado da Cêrca,* Rio de Janeiro, Apec Editôra, 1967.

Campos, Roberto de Oliveira *Ensaios contra a Maré,* Rio de Janeiro, Apec Editôra, 1969.

Dines, Alberto and others *Os idos de Março e a queda em Abril,* Rio de Janeiro, José Alvaro, 1964.

Lambert, Jacques *Os dois Brasis,* São Paulo, Companhia Editôra Nacional, 1970.

Simonsen, Mário Henrique *Brasil 2001,* Rio de Janeiro, Apec Editôra S.A., 1969.

Tamer, Alberto *O Mesmo Nordeste,* São Paulo, Editôra Herder, 1968.

Valverde, Orlando and Vergolino Dias, Catharina *A rodovia Belém-Brasília: estudo de geografia regional,* Rio de Janeiro, Fundação IBGE, Instituto Brasileiro de Geografia, 1967.

Index